The challenge of violence

The challenge of violence

Edited by Derek Richter

Ardua Press   PO Box No. 7   Tadworth Surrey

First published in 1972

Printed in Great Britain by the
Northumberland Press Ltd Gateshead
Bound by Richard Clay (The Chaucer Press) Ltd Bungay
For the Ardua Press Tadworth Surrey.

1072

Contents

5

Preface

There is a common dislike of violence and war, but little agreement on what we should do about it or what practical steps we can take. There is also little communication on the subject between people in different walks of life. The aim of this book is to bring together some of the diversity of different viewpoints in people living in different countries and engaged in different fields of work. A general introductory chapter is followed by two studies of the immediate causes of violence in special trouble spots: they are written by a professor fresh from the US university campus riots and an Irish journalist with first-hand experience of the trouble in Belfast. War can be regarded as a kind of insanity: attention is therefore given to psychiatric aspects. Since faulty upbringing seems to be at the heart of the problem, further chapters deal with educational factors and the concept of maturity. A scientist discusses the international arms race and a housewife the problem of what women can do. Finally a senior statesman and lawyer considers the kind of social organization we should aim at to reduce the risk of violence and war. All have given thought to the problem of war and in particular to the question: What is there that the ordinary person can do about it?

Proceeds from the sale of the book will go to Amnesty International, which is one of the younger and more successful of

the organizations working in the field. One chapter deals with
their work.

Derek Richter
Deans Cottage
Walton-on-the-Hill
Surrey

Contributors

Eric Baker

Eric Baker, M.A., M.Ed. studied in the Universities of Cambridge and Edinburgh. He is currently Head of the Department of Social Science at the North East London Polytechnic. He is Chairman of the British Section of Amnesty International and a member of the International Executive Committee. He contributed to *Alternatives to War and Peace* (1963).

Alan Bestic

Alan Bestic is a non-Catholic Irishman whose mother is from Belfast and whose father was from Dublin. At 17, he joined the staff of *The Irish Times*. Later he moved to *The Irish Press*, *The People*, then *The Evening Standard* and ultimately *The Daily Herald*. Ten years ago he became a freelance journalist. He is the author of a number of books, including *Turn Me On, Man*, *The Importance of Being Irish*, and *Praise the Lord and Pass the Contribution* (1971).

William Gerald Burrows

Prof. W. G. Burrows qualified in medicine at Toronto. During World War II he was on active service with the Royal Canadian Navy Volunteer Reserve. He received his Psychiatric Training in the United States and in England, and later held posts in Canada and California. He is currently Professor of

9

Psychiatry at Omaha, Nebraska. His qualifications include M.D., L.M.C.C., C.R.C.P.(C), D.P.M., F.R.C.P.(C), F.A.P.A. and F.A.C.P.

Robin Clarke

After reading science at Cambridge, Robin Clarke joined the London office of *Encyclopaedia Britannica*. He was editor of *Science Journal* from 1964 until 1971. His publications include *The Diversity of Man* (1964), *We All Fall Down; the Prospect of Chemical and Biological Warfare* (1968) and *The Science of War and Peace* (1971).

Frances Howland Elliott

Dr. Frances Elliott, M.A., Ph.D., studied chemistry at Mt. Holyoke College and at Smith College, Northampton, Mass. After teaching for two years she obtained a Ph.D. at McGill University, Montreal, and engaged for several years in biochemical research in the Allan Memorial Institute. She has published a number of scientific papers. She is married, with three children and one grandchild. Recently she has taken up the study of art and she has held two exhibitions of her work. She is a Vice-president of the Voice of Women.

Geraldine Lack

Born and educated in China at a missionary school, Geraldine Lack studied English and Education at Sydney University, Australia. After ten years' teaching in England she was appointed Headmistress of Portsmouth Northern Secondary School, then in 1946 Headmistress of Rosebery County School, where she remained until her retirement in 1969. She was Senior Walter Hines Page Scholar to the USA in 1957; Delegate to the Commonwealth Education Conference in 1964; Member of Sir John Maud's Committee enquiring into the management of Local Government in 1964-7. Awarded the C.B.E. in 1968.

David MacSweeney

Dr. David MacSweeney, M.A., M.B., B.S., D.P.M., read Experimental Psychology at Cambridge. He held a student research fellowship at Harvard in 1962 and graduated from St. Thomas's Hospital Medical School, London, in 1965. He joined the M R C Neuropsychiatry Unit at Carshalton in 1967 and is currently engaged in research in schizophrenia and drug addiction. He is Lecturer in psychology, University of London School of Extramural Studies. He played international Rugby for Ireland and captained Cambridge University in 1960.

Derek Richter

Dr. Derek Richter, Ph.D., M.R.C.P., F.R.C.Psych., is Director of the Neuropsychiatry Unit of the Medical Research Council at Carshalton and Epsom, Surrey. He has worked as Visiting Professor at the Menninger Foundation, Kansas and at the Mount Sinai Hospital Medical School, New York. His publications include *Perspectives in Neuropsychiatry* (1950), *Schizophrenia – Somatic Aspects* (1957), *Comparative Neurochemistry* (1964) and *Aspects of Learning and Memory* (1966).

Geoffrey Vickers

Sir Geoffrey Vickers served as an infantry officer through the first world war, in which he won the V C. He became a solicitor and practised as a partner in a well-known City of London firm. In 1940 he was re-commissioned, and after a year of special employment as a soldier, became deputy director-general of the Ministry of Economic Warfare in charge of economic intelligence and a member of the Joint Intelligence Committee of the Chiefs of Staff. He was knighted for his war services in 1946. After the war he joined the National Coal Board, first as legal adviser and then as the member in charge of man-power, training, education, welfare and health. Since then, he has devoted himself to study, writing and lecturing, largely in the U S A and Canada, in the fields of management, government and health, especially mental health and public health. He has published many papers and six books, including *The Art of Judgment* (1965) and *Freedom in a Rocking Boat* (1970). He has been a member of many public and professional bodies, including the Medical Research Council, the Councils of The Law Society, the British Institute of Management, the Royal Institute of International Affairs and the London Transport Board, and has held industrial directorships. He was for fifteen years Chairman of the Research Committee of the Mental Health Research Fund.

Psychiatric aspects of violence
Derek Richter

1 The problem of violence

At the present time there is widespread concern about the extent of violence in the world. In the United States there were 4 300 bombings in the 15 months before April 1970, with 40 killed, 384 injured and $23 millions in damage. Some 20 policemen were assassinated. The war in Vietnam has spread to Cambodia, while India and the Middle East have provided Russians and Americans with testing grounds for arms in the rapidly developing armaments race. The cost is staggering in financial terms, but in waste of effort and spiritual frustration the cost is higher still. Young people react with horror and shame from the things their elders are asking them to do. The old answers – 'to save the country from communism', 'to preserve the American way of life' – have grown hollow. Many rebel against the Establishment and protest. Some try to escape by joining the 'drop-outs', while others still struggle to find reason in an insane world. But for many there is no real escape: they find themselves caught up in a state of disillusionment, hating the world they live in and estranged from society, but forced to conclude that 'there is nothing anybody can do about it'.

Must we accept violence and war as a normal expression of human nature, a product of our innate aggressiveness, inevit-

13

able for all time? Is this a normal pattern of human behaviour, or a pathological reflection of a sick society? Is it something we must learn to tolerate or something we can hope to overcome? And if we want to do something about it, can anything be achieved by peaceful means, or must violence be used to remedy violence, risking an even greater holocaust?

These are questions that some of us find hard to answer, questions for which we are perhaps ill prepared. It has been said that wars begin in the minds of men. If that is so, do they begin in healthy or in perverted minds? And if the latter, is this then a problem for psychiatry? It seems at least worth while to follow this line of thought and enquire whether there are any aspects of the problem in which psychiatry has anything to offer. Psychiatric thinking has been influenced in recent years by the ideas of Lorenz[1], Tinbergen[2] and others who have studied the aggressive behaviour of animals in their natural surroundings. It is doubtful to what extent aggression in animals is comparable to that in man, but it may be useful nevertheless to consider possible parallels between certain types of animal and human behaviour. This general approach can also serve as a conceptual framework in which to consider the mechanisms leading to individual and group violence in human communities. Another aspect of the problem with psychiatric implications is the use of solitary confinement, torture and other procedures in the 'brain-washing' of political prisoners. Finally, at an international level, there are questions relating to the concept of world citizenship and mental health in a world community.

2 Normal and pathological aggression

In human society, as in communities of social animals, we can recognize two basically different types of interaction which may be described as (a) competitive and (b) co-operative in kind. Co-operative interactions can be regarded as an extension of the early relationships within the family, as in suckling, grooming, nest-building, hunting and the rearing of young. They are associated with mutual attraction, mutual trust and mutual gain. Competitive interactions also start in early life. They are seen, for example, in the competition of littermates for warmth, and for the nipple. The basic behaviour in such competitive interactions is often aggression, defined simply as unprovoked attack or threat of attack. This is evident in the rough and tumble of the playtime skirmishing in a litter of puppies or kittens as they establish their 'pecking order' or order of dominance. In the young, such aggression appears to be a normal way of exploring the environment and establishing relations with the others in the outside world. It may have survival value in securing an advantage when food or other rewards are in short supply; but in competitive interactions one party is always the loser and any individual gain is at another's expense. Competitive confrontations are thus more appropriate in relation to an outsider than to those within the favoured family group; they tend to be associated with reactions of anger or fear.

Although children can be co-operative, they are also often aggressive. Thus, it is not unusual for small boys to be wielding sticks or throwing stones, and the sight of any small creature – an insect, a bird or a duck on a pond – can be a signal for attack. The joy of achieving a successful hit is free from any sign of remorse. It is not that young children are intentionally cruel: in exercising aggression they are acting simply in the way they are made, and only as they mature do they learn the meaning of cruelty and learn to consider others, besides themselves. Left to themselves they will soon be playing Cowboys and Indians or similar games, and out of the occasional arguments and fights a 'pecking order' will often emerge. But as in the lower animals, serious injuries are rare and a threat alone is often sufficient to establish the order of dominance.

If some show of overt aggression is normal and healthy in the young, it is regarded as abnormal if excessive or if inappropriately expressed, as in the temper tantrums of the spoiled, over-jealous child or the destructiveness of the child who has been too repressed. Excessive or uncontrolled aggression is found, often associated with developmental defects of the temporal lobes of the brain, in children suffering from a disorder known as the 'hyperkinetic syndrome'.

Of special interest are the changes during the transition from childhood to maturity. With maturation there comes an increasing awareness of other people and a growing appreciation of their needs and rights. As the field of consciousness expands, the selfish, competitive viewpoint of the young child gives way to one in which a place must be found for concepts such as 'fair play' and 'fair shares'. At the same time competitive inter- action tends to be replaced by a willingness to co-operate; and co-operative relationships extend increasingly to outsiders be- yond the narrow confines of the immediate family circle or tribe. By the time he reaches adult age a person has normally learned to control his aggressive inclinations and channel them into socially acceptable forms of activity. He may compete in commerce, join the competitive rat-race of professional life or compete in mating behaviour or in games. He may even com- pete in non-conformity or in trying to shock the conventional. In some people, such as the over-exacting parent or the tyranni- cal boss, aggression takes a more militant form; and we regard this as deviating from the normal pattern. Duelling, which was common in the past, is no longer tolerated as an outlet for aggression in civilized countries today, but there are still com- munities where personal violence is accepted in certain forms and there are even backwaters where it is possible for occasional duelling to survive. In 1967 two French Deputies took part in an affair of honour which was widely reported in the press. Apparently a M. Deffere called M. Ribière a congenital cretin, and this led M. Ribière to challenge M. Deffere to a duel. If the aim was to show that he was not a cretin a challenge seemed hardly the best way, for M. Deffere was known to be a skilled swordsman, while M. Ribière had no experience of handling a sword. However the elegant photographs of the duellists in action, which appeared in the press, showed both to have departed from the French code of honour to the extent of cover- ing up their chests. The current reaction was to congratulate both on thus avoiding the greatest danger of French duelling, catching a cold.

Today we can afford to laugh at duelling, but not so long ago it was no laughing matter, for not only were many killed, but many more were forced to risk their lives for little or no reason by the bullies who went around, ready to prove their skill by picking a quarrel with anyone who looked like easy game. Men had to carry swords to defend themselves also from the footpads and armed gangs that haunted the city streets. It is easily forgotten that even up to the beginning of the eighteenth

16

century personal violence was so common as to be regarded almost as part of the natural order of things. There were few at that time who would venture alone in the streets of London at night. The change towards the conditions of personal freedom that we now enjoy was achieved, not through violent protest, but through the efforts of a great many ordinary people who influenced public opinion first towards demanding, and then towards co-operating with, an effective force of police. In 1712, the year when Parliament rejected a bill to abolish duelling, the city constabulary was notoriously corrupt; but with the establishment of the Marine Police in 1798 and then the Metropolitan Police in 1829 the streets of London became safe to walk in. By 1850 public opinion had brought an end to duelling as well.

The individual pattern of aggressive behaviour depends on the environment and it is clearly something that is learned, but there is evidence that aggressive behaviour is also influenced to some extent by hereditary factors. Thus, in some animal species the male is more aggressive than the female, which suggests that aggression is influenced by the sex chromosomes; aggressive behaviour can also be increased artificially under certain conditions by injecting extracts of the male sex glands. In some individuals with the XYY chromosomal abnormality uncontrolled aggression has been reported to occur in association with mental retardation and other signs of defective maturation of the brain. An interesting light was thrown on the matter by the discovery that aggressive behaviour depends on the activity of a small nucleus about the size of an almond, situated in the temporal lobe of the brain. Removal of this 'amygdaloid nucleus' in the monkey eliminates dominance-seeking behaviour and makes even the most tyrannical old male become docile and kindly disposed towards his wives. In recent years patients presenting with intractable aggression have been treated surgically by making cuts through the white matter of the temporal lobes or severing nerve connexions in that region. The results reported at the Second International Conference on Psychosurgery (1970) at Copenhagen from brain operations of this kind were generally regarded as favourable. Of the 200-odd patients so treated, some were previously so violent or aggressive that before surgery their families had to keep them under constant watch, sometimes with police help, whereas after treatment they showed calm behaviour with no need for special care.

Abnormal aggression in the adult is found in cases of brain damage, in drug addiction, in a form of 'psychomotor' epilepsy and in certain kinds of mental illness. Special interest attaches to a group described as 'aggressive psychopaths', many of whom end up sooner or later in prison. Hill and Watterson[3] who studied such a group found them to consist mainly of physically energetic young adults, athletic in build, many of whom had committed crimes of violence. As a group, they tended to be emotionally unstable and liable to outbursts of impulsive behaviour. They were for the most part heavy sleepers and their sexual activity, which was often excessive, sometimes took an aggressive form. They tended to show a lack of consideration or a callous indifference to the feelings of other people and frequently they were anti-social in behaviour. In some cases compulsive risk-taking was a striking feature. Of special interest is the observation that in a high proportion of aggressive psychopaths the electrical activity of the brain is abnormal in type and shows features characteristic of immaturity. This suggests a failure in the normal processes of maturation of the brain.

The individuals described as psychopaths often show in an exaggerated form traits which are common in ordinary people, and since it is hard to define the boundaries between the normal and the pathological it is not uncommon for psychopaths to find their way into public life where they may reach positions of power and influence. They turn up, for example, among fraudulent share-pushers and company promoters, and even in politics. In view of the harm they can do it is clearly desirable that the signs and symptoms of psychopathy should be more widely known, so that individual psychopaths can be recognized before they have gone too far.

3 Organized violence

Co-operation and competition are opposite types of behaviour, but each has survival value in the appropriate situation and often a delicate balance is maintained between them. Thus in the hunting pack there is co-operation up to the moment of the kill, but then there may be competition and fighting over the sharing of the spoils. A common pattern of interaction is that in which members of a group learn to co-operate with each other, but at the same time compete with those outside the group. This 'tribal' pattern of behaviour was studied by Jane Goodall in troops of chimpanzees, who were co-operative within their own troop, but showed aggressive behaviour towards members of other troops. In human society parallels can be seen in the behaviour patterns of family groups, gangs, clans, religious sects, tribes and other more complex organizations. One requirement of the tribal pattern of behaviour is that those outside the co-operating group should be recognizable as 'outsiders'. Social animals commonly recognize outsiders by their clan smells: in human communities the smallest difference in language, origin, colour or creed is sufficient for the purpose. The pattern of co-operation within and competition without is likely to continue so long as there is an advantage to be gained by those inside who maintain it; and since co-operation is nearly always advantageous, the tribal pattern is a highly persistent one.

The joining up of individuals into groups brings new forces into play. Group loyalty implies a partial sacrifice of individual liberty in the interests of the group, but the individual gains a sense of 'belonging' and a new identity with a feeling of increased personal security. Generally the weaker members benefit from association with the stronger and they are able to achieve things together which they could not do alone. The factors determining the ethical behaviour of the group are not easily defined. We know that under some conditions, as when the group feels threatened, a type of mob psychology can come into play. When a mob of angry or frustrated people are 'out for trouble' the more brutal members tend to come to the top and take the lead. Reason then ceases to function and almost anything may happen. Under such conditions a lynch gang will commit atrocities that would not easily be committed by individual members on their own. This is true also of the gangs of city youths who engage in 'paki-bashing', 'queer-bashing', 'jew-baiting' and similar activities; but here we may be dealing with an aspect of immaturity in youths who have failed to develop a real sense of values and have turned to violence as an escape from boredom. However, against such examples of pathological behaviour can be cited many others where a group association has enabled individuals to rise to acts of heroism and devotion, or to give of their very best. Clearly there are other factors, and especially leadership, which are important in determining the behaviour of a group. It would appear that group violence, like individual violence, can occur as a reaction to what is felt to be a provocation, but we cannot conclude from this that it is part of human nature for adult human beings to attack each other under normal conditions without due cause.

Groups of social animals sometimes act towards a variant in ways that appear to be cruel. A mutant differing slightly from the rest in colour or in form may be put to death or excluded from the group. This may have survival value in getting rid of individuals that are malformed or diseased. Human society is generally tolerant of the harmless variant, such as the imbecile, but not of the variant who is regarded with suspicion as being in some way foreign to the group. This is seen in the treatment accorded in former times to the leper, the epileptic and the witch: it can be seen today in the cruelty of certain groups towards the 'blackleg' or the 'odd-man-out'.

Some sections of mankind are believed to have evolved from a primitive type of hunting existence in which survival depended largely on the ability to kill – killing for food and killing for sport or to develop skill. Most predatory animals kill only for food and rarely if ever kill others of their own kind, but in primitive human tribes we find men killing, not only game and beasts of prey, but sometimes also killing members of other tribes who might compete for the hunting grounds. Something of this kind continues to this day among the primitive hunting tribes in backward corners of the world, as in the Amazon basin in Brazil, where the members of such tribes are hostile to all outside the tribe and ready even to kill at sight. Lorenz[1] suggested a parallel in claiming that 'man's social organization is similar to that of rats which, like humans, are social and peaceful beings within their clans, but devils to all who do not belong to their own community'. However as Carrighar[4] has pointed out, separate clans of rats will quickly learn to live together in peace, provided that they are not confined in too small a space. The suggested analogy is therefore misleading in its implications.

The habit of certain groups of human beings to live by killing and plundering each other is apparent in the history of our own ancestors in the Western world. Fighting and piracy seem to have been among the customs of the Goths, the Huns, the Vikings and of many border tribes at the edges of the more civilized communities in the past. Ethnologists have discussed a number of factors that might account for the different behaviour of animals and man over killing their own kind – the more lethal nature of human weapons, the ability of men to kill at a distance, the relative lack of gestures of submission, the combination of dominance-seeking and territorial aggression. Without attempting a detailed analysis it is clear that, although widespread, fighting is by no means the only way of life in human communities: there have always been many who preferred to live in peace. While anyone may fight if sufficiently provoked, unprovoked attack resembles rather a habit of the kind that has to be learned – a bad habit perhaps, but not attributable to a specific 'killer instinct' or 'fighting instinct' unique to man.

An important derivative of the tribal pattern of organization is the Establishment, which is a characteristic feature of the modern national State. The Establishment has no formal constitution and no address: it is made up of a network of interdependent hierarchies extending through the community and held together by strings of mutual dependence, family connexions and old-school ties. Prominent in the Establishment are the leaders in finance and industry, and it includes also the War Office and Treasury, armed forces and police, judiciary, churches and the government of the day as well as professional bodies of various kinds. The balance of power in the Establishment differs in different countries, depending on the order of dominance of the different hierarchies concerned. Their relations may be indicated by posing the question: with which of the other hierarchies is it most essential to keep on good terms? On this basis, in the military dictatorships the armed forces are the dominant controlling group which none of the other hierarchies can afford to offend. In the democracies the financial and industrial interests are generally in the lead. Yet no one of the constituent hierarchies ever has it all their own way. The influence of the churches has receded in most parts of the world, but it is still important in the Roman Catholic and

Moslem states. Professional bodies such as doctors and teachers come relatively low in the order of dominance. The government may be elected by the people: but since the Establishment controls the mass media, the Treasury and the main sources of financial support, it generally has the last word, for no government can afford for long to offend the whole array of established power. Events are often blamed on governments, but the governments are mostly the servants of Establishments: and in the most important things instead of government by the people, it tends to be government by lobby.

Every Establishment contains individuals with a social conscience, but the primary aim of Establishments is generally that of looking after themselves; and they maintain their power by applying the age-old tribal principle – co-operation within and competition with those outside. The separation within the same country is maintained by differences of many kinds, as in occupation, income, language ('U' or 'Non-U'), class, training or school. The first requirement of the Establishment is to maintain law and order, so as to avoid subversive change: hence in the Police States the excessive allocation of power and privilege to the police.

Trouble starts when an Establishment goes too far and, taking advantage of its relative strength, deprives the ordinary people of what they regard as their basic rights. When the invasion of human rights goes so far that many are deprived of their liberty and exploited in a tyrannical way, when people feel threatened and go in fear, then the stage is set for civil violence. The resulting outbursts of violence may be regarded as a form of protest or defiance. The important thing is that in such cases the original provocation stems from aggression on the part of an Establishment which is exploiting the people in its own interests in the familiar tribal way; and we should not regard as aggressors those outside the Establishment who may try to defend themselves.

4 Coercion by torture and imprisonment

At the present time there are more than thirty countries in the world where imprisonment is being used as a political tool, to silence those who have neither used nor advocated violence themselves, but who are politically inconvenient.[5] In some cases

22

imprisonment involves solitary confinement, with ill-treatment of various kinds. Some Establishments are using forced retention in mental hospitals, some are known to use torture, and various methods of 'brain-washing' are employed. Tyranny of this kind must inevitably produce adverse effects, and at this point it may be relevant to consider more closely the psychiatric implications of violence of this kind.

Older studies of criminals serving life sentences showed that a high proportion were mentally deranged: this suggested that long term imprisonment can lead to mental illness. However criminals who receive life sentences tend to be mentally abnormal anyway. Wilmanns[6] concluded that the criminal career and imprisonment are both the result of a pre-existing mental derangement which merely becomes more manifest in prison. To get reliable evidence on this point we need to know the previous mental state of the prisoners and avoid observer bias in judging the effects. The reliability of the findings is relatively high in observations on the effects of imprisonment on prisoners of war, since men accepted in the armed forces must generally have a certain degree of mental stability. Many taken as prisoners by the Japanese during World War II were subjected for long periods to the grossest forms of brutality. They were humiliated, beaten up, overworked, undernourished and forced to suffer in many cases from the effects of incidental infections and vitamin deficiencies. Particularly striking to the medical observer was their dull, bitter, apathetic frame of mind. It must be remembered that the men we saw were only the survivors: we had no real record of the many others who had died. The cause of death was in most cases ill-defined: the prisoners themselves called it 'give-up-itis'. In the words of Wolff[7]: 'The prisoner simply became apathetic, listless, neither ate nor drank, helped himself in no way, stared into space and finally died.' While physical symptoms were always present, it may be noted that the mental symptoms corresponded in some respects to those seen in patients suffering from a depressive illness.

Particularly informative are the American statistics comparing the effects of imprisonment in Europe, where conditions were relatively tolerable, with those in the Pacific area, where they were particularly bad. It was found that by the end of the war, less than one per cent of the US soldiers captured in

23

Europe had died in prison, whereas more than 30 per cent of those imprisoned in the Pacific area had died. A further investigation six years later showed that the number of deaths in the intervening period in ex-prisoners from the Far East was three times that in ex-prisoners from Europe. Moreover, twice the expected number died from suicide and three times the expected number died as a result of 'accidents'. These figures give evidence that some of the effects of ill-treatment in prison persisted for a number of years. The high incidence of deaths from suicide and 'accidents' suggests that mental as well as physical factors were involved.

Further evidence of the effects of ill-treatment are to be found in some of the old reports on the slave trade. Here again the original slaves can be accepted as of normal mentality, and observer bias was minimal, since the reports were eye-witness accounts made for business reasons at the request of traders interested only in the commercial aspects of the matter. The usual procedure for obtaining slaves was that the trader, bringing trade-gin and other merchandise, approached a native African chief, who ordered out an armed force, made a night march, attacked a village just before dawn, killed those who resisted and carried off the rest in irons. They were then handed over to the trader, who drove them down to the coast, where they were kept in dungeons and branded ready for shipping. On board, the slaves were packed down in the hold in chains like herrings in a cask. There were no proper sanitary arrangements and many refused to eat; but by means of an instrument thrust down the throat they were forced to take the meals of horse-beans on which they were fed. In spite of the care exercised by the traders, there were often heavy losses on the long voyage to the New World and this was therefore a cause for concern. To quote Winwood Reade:[8] 'Such was the obstinacy of these savage creatures, that many of them sulked themselves to death; and sometimes, when indulged with an airing on deck, the ungrateful wretches would jump overboard, and, as they sank, waved their hands in triumph at having made their escape'. The traders took due note of this and, since exercise was required for physical health, they ordered that, instead of being exercised on deck, the slaves should be made to jump up and down in their chains, a procedure encouraged by the use of a whip known as the 'cat'. After arrival at their destination the business of breaking them in commenced in earnest; but the further losses from suicide were then no longer the traders' concern. Those who still failed to recognize their good fortune in being brought to a Christian country, and tried to escape, were hunted with bloodhounds; some were flogged and hung alive in chains. For more serious offences some were burned alive. The frequent references in these reports to refusal to eat, neglect of the person, apathy, suicide and 'sulking to death' give independent evidence that, even in a normal population, imprisonment under adverse conditions can produce serious mental as well as physical harm.

The use of torture in the witch trials. The use of torture to force people to do things against their will is as old as recorded history. The methods used have varied to some extent in different countries and at different times. In primitive communities, beating, binding, burning, cutting off ears or hands and similar methods have generally sufficed; but in Europe, particularly in the trials of witches conducted by the courts of the Holy Inquisition and in the Ecclesiastical Courts, the methods used were more refined. They included crushing the fingers with the thumb-screw, stretching on the rack or ladder to dislocate the shoulder bones, scalding with boiling fat, burning in the heated iron chair, and crushing the legs in vices (known as Spanish boots). In some courts those who confessed were permitted to be strangled before they were burned, but many were burned alive without this concession, and that was true of all the witches condemned in Italy and Spain.

The long verbatim reports of the witches' trials provide a large body of factual evidence about the effects of torture, and something may still be learned from them. The procedures to be used in the trials were laid down in the famous *Malleus Maleficarum* first printed in 1486 and republished in thirteen new editions up to 1669. It owed its authority mainly to a papal bull given by Pope Innocent VIII. The procedures for examination are given there in detail. After bringing the prisoner to the torture chamber the jailers prepared the implements of torture and the prisoner was stripped bare. The judge tried first to persuade the prisoner to confess, but if he refused he was bound and the various stages of torture were commenced. The interrogations were continued daily for several days using tortures of increasing severity until the last, which was kept for forcing the prisoner to name his friends and accomplices. After each torture the victim was warmed and clothed, so that he might recover sufficiently to endure the next day's torture without losing consciousness too soon. Many died under torture and often a doctor was brought in to revive a victim who seemed near death. It was strictly enjoined that in between the interrogations the prisoner must be kept under constant observation to prevent his committing suicide.

The central feature of the tortures was the infliction of physical pain, but it was recognized that some prisoners were broken down more readily if pain was combined with humiliation, fatigue and fear. That is illustrated also by the 'pig torture' which was used at a later date in the interrogation of tribesmen on the North West frontier of India. It was found that hardy prisoners who were contemptuous of yielding to physical pain, could be persuaded by the threat of forcing them to touch a pig; for according to their religious beliefs merely to touch this unclean animal would involve them in the direst penalties in the world to come. It would appear that in the witch trials the torture chamber filled with elaborate mechanical instruments served not only for the infliction of pain, but also to wear the victim down by anxiety and fear.

In the reports of the reactions of the prisoners it is striking that, whereas some suffered terribly and soon lost consciousness, others showed little response and appeared to come through almost unscathed. Was this attributable to bravery, or because different people vary in their sensitivity to pain? It is generally accepted that some people are hypersensitive, but it is not always appreciated that at the other extreme there are many who are relatively *in*sensitive to pain. There are even some who have never experienced any feeling of pain at all in their lives.[9] This condition, known to neurologists as 'pain asymbolia', is disadvantageous in ordinary life, since pain helps us to avoid injury. While a complete absence of pain sensation is rare, it is probably true that many ordinary people are somewhat 'bovine' in their reactions and relatively insensitive to pain. The point is of interest because it may help us to under-

26

stand, not only why some people can tolerate so much ill treatment, but also why many people are so indifferent to pain and suffering in others. Those who are hypersensitive sometimes assume that others are as sensitive to pain as they are themselves. They must then take a somewhat depressing view of 'man's inhumanity to man'. The view that many people are relatively insensitive may enable one to take a kindlier view of the world and to feel that the task of combating ill treatment is not so hopeless as otherwise it might seem.

Patients suffering from certain forms of mental dissociation ('hysterical anaesthesias') are sometimes found to have a loss of pain sensation in a limb; and anaesthesia to pain can be produced by hypnosis in many people. It seems unlikely that the prisoners in the witch trials were able to avail themselves of hypnosis, but some of them were highly suggestible, hysterical types; and it is not impossible that in some of them mental dissociation played a certain part in diminishing the appreciation of pain.

With the hindsight we possess today, it is hard to understand how reputedly learned people such as judges and bishops could go on believing in the value of confessions extracted under torture and could continue to support the validity of the torture trials. The *Malleus Maleficarum*, which was the bible of the courts, is a monument of error and irrational thinking: the witnesses were repeatedly shown to be corrupt and yet, because of the forced confessions, more and more were named as accomplices and few who were brought to trial ever managed to escape. Refusal to confess meant torture, and to retract a confession meant burning alive. Much of the blame can be laid on the Church, but, to be fair, one must remember the part played by ignorance and superstition in the common people, who blamed the witches for every misfortune that befell them. There were always a few who spoke out bravely against the torture trials, but to show lenience towards the witches involved the danger of being named as an accomplice; and there were few who were willing to take the risk.

A major force in ending the torture trials was the opposition from public-spirited individuals, but in the end what greatly influenced public opinion was the disclosure of dishonesty and corruption in the informers and witnesses. It was found that there were informers who, for a consideration, would name almost anyone as a witch. Another factor in bringing the trials to an end was ridicule. In 1683 it is recorded that a courageous Quaker judge, William Penn, faced with an old Swedish woman charged with witchcraft asked: 'Art thou a witch? Hast thou ridden through the air on a broomstick?' The confused old woman said that she had, whereupon Penn remarked tersely that there were no traffic regulations forbidding this form of transport: she had every right to ride a broomstick if she wished. With that he promptly dismissed the case.

Brain-washing and confessions of guilt. Coming now to the procedures used in more recent years, at the time of the Korean war it was a surprise to many people that American prisoners of war were making public confessions of spying, engaging in bacterial warfare and other activities known to be untrue. Moreover some of them appeared to have a genuine belief in the truth of their false confessions. The propaganda value of these spurious confessions was undoubtedly very great, and skilful use was made of them.

The idea that the mental change associated with the confessions was obtained by a secret process of 'brain-washing' was reported in the press as if it represented something entirely new. It was hinted that mental conversion was achieved by a highly scientific process of conditioning, applied by a specially trained body of psychiatrists. However the careful investigations of workers such as Hinkle and Wolff[10] showed that that was not so. One or two of the methods employed, such as the use of electrical appliances and drugs, were relatively new; but in general the methods used today for 'brain-washing' are very old. They are in fact based on those previously used in Czarist times by the Russian secret police and earlier still in the witch trials.

As applied to political prisoners, the first step is generally sudden arrest and solitary confinement, with no reason being given and no communication of any kind being allowed. This normally produces a condition of frustration and fear, which leads to a state of anxiety. As the days pass and no change of any kind takes place, the initial bewilderment gives way to a state of alert expectancy. The prisoner may attempt to fratern-

28

ize with the jailer or try on other tricks. But gradually, as every attempt at communication fails, anxiety increases and sleep is impaired. The result is a state of endless boredom and fatigue. The prisoner becomes jumpy and irritable, and then a state of general dejection begins to develop. According to Hinkle and Wolff[10] the isolation associated with solitary confinement is the main factor in producing this change. The prison officials selected to do the interrogation watch with interest as the symptoms develop in a predictable way and the prisoner becomes, as they call it, 'acclimatized'. Gradually, as the weeks go by, all hope disappears. The prisoner begins to neglect his person and may soil himself. At times he may weep or mutter aloud; he develops a vacant facial expression and the mental state is one of dazed depression and docility. In this condition, which is generally reached in four to six weeks, the prisoner is highly suggestible; and in his confused mental state the distinction between 'true' and 'might be true' easily becomes blurred. It is then time for the procedures of interrogation to commence.

Interrogation generally takes the form of demanding a confession. No specific charge is made at first and no crimes are mentioned, but guilt is taken as established. Repeatedly the prisoner is told that only by confessing his crimes and naming his associates can he obtain release. At an appropriate time the hostile questioning may be replaced by an attitude of apparent friendliness. Finally the suggestion of the prisoner's guilt may be reinforced and 're-education' extended by including him in a group of other prisoners who have already confessed and who are hoping to earn their release. Some prisoners are found to be more resistant than others, and that has been observed especially in members of active religious sects. The process of breaking down can then be aided by a number of supplementary procedures. The usual methods are to increase fatigue by long standing, or to produce deprivation of sleep. Some prisoners become delirious and have hallucinations: a prisoner may hear the voice of God telling him to co-operate with his interrogator. Recently attempts have been made to aid this process of mental derangement by administering a hallucinogenic drug such as LSD. While some individuals of exceptional stability may succeed in resisting most of the other procedures, no one can maintain his mental integrity under the influence of a drug of this kind.

The procedures used for breaking down prisoners are not regarded as 'torture' by those who apply them. In many cases physical pain has certainly been used, but the main factor is generally mental stress produced by long-continued isolation, associated with anxiety, fatigue, frustration and fear. As a result of this treatment the prisoner is no longer mentally normal and the statements he may make are as likely to be false as true. Under these conditions he commonly develops a form of mental derangement with symptoms that may include dejection, apathy, fatigue, personal neglect, inability to sleep, thoughts of suicide and feelings of self-reproach and guilt. While in this abnormal mental state a person may not only make an untrue confession, but at the time he may believe in his guilt. The symptoms are similar to those of a depressive illness and it may be regarded as a form of reactive depression.

It need hardly be said that such treatment is mentally as well as physically damaging. An abnormal mental pattern forced to develop in this way is liable to recur again under conditions of stress. This may be the reason for the increased incidence of suicide in ex-prisoners of war in the years after their release from prison. Only in a certain proportion of cases does a prisoner develop a belief in his false confessions and in his personal guilt, and these characteristics soon tend to disappear. However the process may be a painful one.

We have considered the mental state of persons subjected to torture and imprisonment, but what about the mentality of the torturers, and of those in authority, who are ultimately to blame? There are certainly cases where sadism has played a part; but although sadists are common enough, we are told that the interrogator's posts are not easily filled. It is therefore unlikely that sadism is often more than an aggravating factor. In every society it is necessary for laws to be enforced to maintain internal peace; and it is understandable that a government that is weak and operating in a backward country may be unable to maintain the standards expected of a stable government in a modern democratic state. Some of the worst abuses of power are due, in fact, not so much to the unwillingness of the authorities as to their simple inability to control the excesses

30

of those who are supposed to be their servants. Prisons and police are justified so long as they are used to protect the community from crime, but there can be no excuse for their misuse by a small section of the Establishment or by members of a political party as a means of intimidating or destroying those to whom they are politically opposed. Yet that is precisely the situation in several countries at the present day.[5] One can only regard as psychopathic those who are prepared to use torture and solitary confinement in this way.

If the present situation is an unhappy one, at least it is no worse than in former times, when prisoners were publicly crucified, thrown to the lions or thrown to the wolves. A fairly consistent trend is the gradual replacement of such public forms of punishment by methods applied in secret, and concealed. This may be a hopeful sign in indicating that public opposition to torture is more advanced, if those who practise torture are forced to hide and deny their crimes. Galsworthy once remarked that 'the only ultimate sin is cold indifference'. The torturing and imprisonment of political opponents has become increasingly a matter for concern and one can hope that those whose indifference has allowed this evil to persist will come to see that this is something that can no longer be tolerated anywhere in the world.

5 International war

War is not as a rule an isolated event, but a terminal phase in a series of processes often extending over many years. There has been much discussion of the causes of war, and if we are to understand them we must go back to the earliest events which set the processes of war in train. Ethologists have shown that overcrowding can lead to aggressive behaviour in colonies of social animals such as rats; and some people have concluded that population pressure is a major factor in the causation of international war.[11] Before accepting this view there are one or two questions that should be asked. In particular, what population density constitutes overcrowding for man? In many countries people appear to show a preference for living under urban conditions at a relatively high density, but there is little evidence that those who live in the crowded cities are more inclined to war than those in sparsely populated areas. Again, there is little evidence that war is more frequent in countries that are densely populated than in those that are not. Thus it may be questioned whether India, with a population ranging from 100 to 400 per square mile can be regarded as more belligerent than the United States or the U S S R where the population is mainly less than 20 per square mile. It is also unlikely that wars were any less frequent in previous centuries when the overall population of the world was only a fraction of what it is today.

It might be argued that the factor concerned is not the population density alone, but the ratio of population to the means of subsistence, for in most animal species the population at any time is determined largely by the food supply. This has been true in countries such as India and China, where for many centuries periodic famines have been a major factor in population control. Increased competition for food associated with an increase in population can be blamed for many ills, and it might reasonably be expected to lead to aggressive behaviour in the ordinary population. But the ordinary people as a rule have very little to do with making war. And even in times of famine there is rarely a shortage of food among the élite in the controlling section of the Establishment where international affairs are mainly arranged. Military leaders have sometimes called for an increase in population to increase a country's military strength, as in de Gaulle's demand for a hundred million Frenchmen for France. Clearly an adequate supply of troops expendable on the battlefield is one of the requisites for making war: but in modern warfare the size of an army is no longer a measure of its military strength. The evidence therefore suggests that, although overcrowding is socially harmful and undesirable in many ways, other factors are probably more important as determinants of international war.

Lorenz[1] has expressed the opinion that 'military enthusiasm is an instinctive response with a phylogenetically determined releasing mechanism'. One wonders whether he would have held this view if, instead of studying mainly lower vertebrates, he had studied the 'military enthusiasm' of an average group of untrained American conscripts! Analogies can be misleading and, as Boulding[12] has put it, Lorenz's approach is rather like trying to find out something about the jet plane by studying the wheelbarrow. Lorenz is an authority in his own field, and wide publicity has been given to his views, but his speculations on human behaviour have been rightly criticized by ethologists and others as scientifically unsound.[13]

An alternative hypothesis is that wars are mainly products of faulty social systems.[12] In looking for ultimate causes we may ask: Who at the start might hope to gain an advantage from the threat of war? The common people are not as a rule directly concerned with matters of that kind which are generally left to the government. But governments do not act alone: their way of thinking, and generally of acting too, is largely shaped by the Establishment. If we accept that in most countries the Establishment is the main decision-making body and that Establishments are tribally orientated groups which tend to compete with those outside, it is in the nature of things that Establishments should be seeking to gain advantage by competing with one another: and it is hardly surprising if this should sometimes lead to war. On this formulation war is seen as a terminal phase in a confrontation of competitive type which starts when the controlling section of the Establishment in one country comes to believe it is strong enough for some advantage to be gained by making aggressive demands on another. It may be to gain control of oil-fields, mines, food supplies, trade routes or other natural resources, or because of fear of losing some advantage such as profitable markets elsewhere.

The next step in the process is to give power to a government that will play the part in developing military strength by increasing expenditure on armaments, generally in the name of 'national defence'. Nationalistic propaganda is then directed towards conditioning the ordinary people to the idea that the foreigner is not to be trusted and constitutes a threat to them. In this way there is built up a persistent sense of provocation, with a fear of losing territory, losing trade routes, essential supplies, rightful supremacy, 'a place in the sun' or even losing face. Of all the primitive tribal emotions fear is the easiest to evoke and the one most readily turned to violence; and once the scene is set it needs only a small spark to set the conflagration going and stampede the population into war. Many join up and fight for idealistic reasons – 'for King and country', 'to defend the Fatherland', 'because God is on our side', 'because it is a war to end wars' or for some religious pretext: but these are not the reasons of those who originally set the processes of war in motion.

If this picture of events is anywhere near the truth it should be applicable to experience in recent times. In Germany in 1932 the Krupps and other families of industrial tycoons who led the German Establishment were as astute as any comparable group in the world. They were never taken in by the crude beer-hall politics of the Austrian corporal, who shouted defiance at the Allied occupying powers and blamed the Jews for all the troubles of the Reich. But they saw his ability to sway the masses and, calculating that he could serve their purposes, they gave him money and publicity, helped him to establish the ultra-nationalistic National Socialist Party as a political force, and then finally gave them arms and power. They shrugged their shoulders at the excesses of Streicher, Himmler, Goebbels and the rest. How could anyone believe such stuff, and what did it matter anyway if the Nazis killed a few Jews? It suited their purpose well enough to let Hitler rant while building up the military strength of the Reich. What mattered to them was that Hitler and his crowd of Nazi fanatics had no qualms about breaking the binding agreements of the past, overriding the objections of the intellectuals, defaulting on the payment of reparations and so enabling them to escape from the irksome domination of France and the Allied powers. In the end the Nazis may have gone too far and got out of hand, but at the time they served their purpose in freeing Germany from the strangle-hold of reparations and restoring the old borders of the Reich in Czechoslovakia, Austria and the Sudetenland. And now, but a few years after World War II, we find a Germany relatively stronger and wealthier than before and with the same family of industrial tycoons more firmly than ever in power. And the cost? More perhaps than they bargained for in German lives, but still far lower than the cost to the Russians, Jews and other Allied powers. Establishments like to operate behind the scenes and only rarely do they show their hand. Interest therefore attaches to the recent disclosure of pressures, including a bribe of RM 350 000, applied by the German Establishment to persuade a politician to change his allegiance and vote against his own party.

Wars undertaken by other countries appear to have started in a comparable way. The Italian invasion of Ethiopia can be said to have started when the Establishment in Italy, still dominated by the old aristocracy and the Church, and nervous of communist influence, gave money and power to a right-wing Fascist group. The Italians can hardly be regarded as a warlike people and it took a lengthy period for the building up of nationalist sentiment and military strength before they were ready to be pushed into the Ethiopian adventure. A similar story can be found in the Japanese invasion of China. Were the situations very different in the Russian invasion of Finland and Czechoslovakia or the American invasion of Vietnam? The latest British involvement of the kind was the invasion of Suez when, without reference to Parliament or the people, British troops were ordered to attack in secret collusion with the French. The Tory Prime Minister, Anthony Eden, took the blame for the fiasco which ensued, and little was heard at the time of the powerful oil and shipping interests behind the scenes.

The tribal nature of these conflicts is suggested again by the way the propaganda media have been used to put blame on the foreigner. So the British were told of the atrocities of the Germans, the Germans heard of the brutality of the Russians, the Russians learned of the intransigence of the Chinese, the Chinese heard of the cruelty of the Japanese, and the Japanese, mindful of Hiroshima, are told that the Americans are the most brutal race of all. But what is the truth? Are some nations intrinsically more brutal than others? Accepting that cultural traditions vary widely even within the same community, and that where conditions are primitive standards tend to be low, it would appear that every country can throw up people of Nazi mentality as well as kindly liberals and sometimes even saints. Depending on prevailing conditions, sometimes the one and sometimes the other will come to the top and play a dominant role.

Conclusions

Some dismiss as unthinkable the prospect of another world war, now that with nuclear weapons it must mean massive destruction on both sides. Yet the destructiveness of the new weapons gives little reason for believing they will not be used. More nations are joining the 'nuclear club' and, taking things as we find them, it would be strange and something new in history, if the present situation did not end in war.

If war is regarded as an inevitable result of the aggressive instincts inherent in human nature, we are forced to take a pessimistic view; but psychiatric experience indicates that human behaviour is determined by mechanisms more complex than the simple instinctive responses studied in animals. While accepting that an individual can be provoked to violence as an emergency response, and that this can occur with little provocation in the young and immature, it is reasonable to regard unprovoked violence as pathological in a person of mature age. The organized killing at a distance and other performances of modern war can be learned by processes of training or conditioning, but such behaviour is culturally determined and not a simple instinctive response: it is associated especially with the 'tribal' type of social organization. Men can be said to have an aggressive urge to self-expression or self-fulfilment, but only in the psychopath does this take a form which involves the killing or wounding of other people.

If we take the view that war is not inevitable we come at once to the question of how it can be prevented. Here opinions are again divided. Some put their faith in the United Nations and enforcement of international law by an effective force of international police: others see the problem as primarily a moral one and feel the first requirement is some kind of a religious awakening or spiritual rebirth. There is a current feeling that the maintenance of peace cannot safely be left to the authorities, but that it is something in which every citizen should participate, yet what is there that the ordinary person can do? The young activists believe that one should protest or try to overthrow the Establishment by violence, but they generally have little idea of what to put in its place. Whatever view is taken, it is unlikely that war can be ended overnight simply by some magic formula that will somehow immobilize the whole military machine and make all governments change their ways: it is more likely to involve a long-drawn-out struggle continuing for many years. In any case, for many who live in the totalitarian states the immediate problem is not international aggression, but aggression exerted at home by a government which has deprived the ordinary people of their freedom and their rights. Here again there are advocates of violent and non-violent remedies.

There is a tendency to think of peace and war as matters determined by generals and politicians, at a level above the influence of ordinary folk. Yet all wars are stopped sooner or later; and history can provide many examples of wars that were stopped, not by generals or politicians, but by ordinary people who decided for themselves that they had had enough. Thus it was not so much the stalemate on the battlefield as a mutiny in the German navy in 1918 that ended the First World War; and it was a strike of Belgian workers in 1940 that ended Belgian participation in the Second World War. 'Shoot the strikers' was Churchill's reaction at the time, but the strikers won in the end. If wars cannot always be prevented, can they be cut short or can their onset be delayed? To shorten a war even by a day would be an achievement not to be despised.

Ordinary people have a great deal of power if they are prepared first to organize and then to work for effective leadership. Most of the progress made hitherto in working for peace has in fact been made by organizations of various kinds operating locally, nationally and at an international level. Encouraging as an indication of public concern is the increasing membership of voluntary organizations dealing with civil rights, United Nations, amnesty and international law. The importance of effective leadership is shown by the fact that some of the older organizations, which have done excellent work in the past, have now lost their original momentum and gone stale. They continue to hold meetings where resolutions are passed, but otherwise they are not doing very much and they no longer capture the imagination of the young. At the other extreme there are a number of recently formed bodies of young activists in which the leaders are so lacking in judgment and experience that they are in danger of doing more harm than good to the causes they espouse. As well as being active, the leadership clearly needs to be competent and sane. Organization within a profession can also be effective in influencing events. After the occupation of Holland in the Second World War the Nazis decided to mobilize the Dutch medical profession to assist in their programme of extermination by euthanasia of the 'physically or socially unfit'. However, the Dutch doctors were unanimous in refusing to co-operate. When threatened with the revocation of their licences, every doctor threw in his licence, but continued to see his patients as before. The Germans arrested 100 Dutch physicians and tried many other means of persuasion, but the medical profession remained adamant in refusing to co-operate.[14]

Events are influenced to some extent by public opinion and this is something to which all contribute. Public opinion is largely dependent on the general educational level and it is encouraging to find that, in spite of their history of war, the Scandinavian countries, which have the highest educational standards in the world, are also in the lead in promoting international peace. However, improving the level of education does not mean merely indoctrinating others with pacifist ideas, or teaching that children should be deprived of their toy guns: it means working to create conditions in which people can grow up with minds of their own and with a mature appreciation of the needs of other people. How this is best accomplished is still open for discussion, but some will agree with A. S. Neill[15] when he says: 'Fifty years of Summerhill have shown me that free children become, not pacifists, but peaceful, unaggressive folks. Hence I conclude that if all kids were reared in freedom we might have a world of peace. Most people are peaceful, but having been killed emotionally in their cradles by the ideology of the ruling classes ... sex repression, obedience, in short castration, the masses, like sheep, are led to the slaughter, or more often rush into it at the command of any Hitler. Peace depends on abolishing moulding character.... The answer to peace is real freedom, not political but emotional.' Relevant again is Sanderson's plea that instead of the current emphasis on competition in the schools, every opportunity should be given to young people for joining in co-operative ventures, so that they develop the habit of working together with, instead of always competing with, their fellow men.

One major change, which could influence things greatly for the better, is the increase in communication, as radio and television are bringing millions into closer touch with world affairs. Inevitably there are countries where the media are misused for propaganda purposes, but people do not believe all they hear: propaganda often misfires and it may even stimulate some to find out the truth. In the long run such abuses of the media are likely to be less important than their positive educational value; and their impact on world affairs has hardly yet begun. One effect of television, largely unforeseen, is in making the public more aware of the personality of the political leaders for whom they vote. There are cases where a television interview has shown up all too clearly a 'chip on the shoulder', a streak of cruelty, a lack of social conscience, or other characteristics of the power-seeking hawk.

Many people are thinking seriously about international problems for the first time, and this may be a factor in the worldwide outbreaks of student unrest. Young people feel deeply about the evils of war and they are sensitive to the apparent lack of concern in the world. It is intolerable to them, when people are being killed, to see those in authority apparently ignoring the issues that really matter. If they protest, it is because they are looking for something better. They may not know all the answers, but they are learning, perhaps the hard way, that there is really no short-cut – that a better kind of world can be achieved only by hard work, and that the price of peace is eternal vigilance. At least it is encouraging to find that even in the USSR, despite the propaganda, many students are thinking for themselves, rejecting the Party lines and demanding the freedom of the press. The need for an international newspaper, giving uncensored statements from both sides, has often been discussed. The *International Herald Tribune* published in Paris, which Pulitzer originally intended to fulfil this role, is now about as international as the Stars and Stripes; and it seems that we must wait for a truly international newspaper until there is the necessary financial support. In the meantime a noteworthy contribution is that of the cartoonists, in their skilful use of ridicule to deflate the romantic schoolboy idea of war as an affair of commando adventures and heroics. It is encouraging that in South Africa and elsewhere the press have taken a courageous stand in opposing censorship: the average pressman's urge to spill out the truth seems to be something that not even the most tyrannical dictator can ever entirely manage to cure.

Another factor favouring peace is the world-wide spread of scientific knowledge. Science is sometimes blamed because it has been used to develop military weapons, but the argument is hardly fair, for there is little that cannot be misused by those who have a mind to. The important thing is that the language of science is international, and scientists from different countries can meet and exchange views with a freedom that is denied to politicians or diplomats. Moreover the whole scientific approach is one of questioning, examining and testing, an attitude of mind especially needed in dealing with international affairs.

Psychiatrists have been mainly concerned with treating the mentally sick and they have generally had little to say on wider issues such as peace and war: but in 1948, three years after the Second World War, a group of leading psychiatrists and social scientists from 46 countries met in London to discuss the problem of 'Mental Health and World Citizenship'. The proceedings of the meeting were published at length in the form of a remarkable document,[16] much of which is as relevant today as when it was written. It was pointed out that the idea of world citizenship is neither novel nor remote: the move towards a world community accords with the general trend of history in which the loyalty of the individual has extended, first from his family to his feudal lord, then to a regional prince and finally to a king or ruler of a composite national state. Countries such as France, Italy, Germany and the USA have all been formed by the joining up of smaller states, and the logical extension of this process is the formation of a single world community. To some the idea of world citizenship is completely visionary, but as Brock Chisholm put it, 'visionary is a term of reproach only if the vision is not followed by action'. Although still far from being a political reality, nevertheless in a more limited sense world citizenship is already in existence; for already there is a growing body of people who in their thinking and in their sympathies have transcended the outworn concepts of nationality and become in a real sense citizens of the world.

The social scientists at the London meeting drew attention to the primitive level of much of the current thinking on international relations – the tendency for example to personify communities and treat them as if they were individuals. It was noted that the world is beset by international tensions, suspicions,

40

prejudices, hostility and fear: we have the knowledge as to how these unhealthy attitudes arise in a community and how they can be replaced by attitudes of friendship and co-operation which are natural to all human beings; yet almost nowhere have the principles of mental health been brought to bear on the crucial problems which confront mankind. A major difficulty is the widespread ignorance of the different values of people in different parts of the world. What does the average American or European know, for example, of the things that matter most to the average Chinese, a people so recently emancipated from the feudal state that they have never known the freedoms now taken for granted in the West. Even at home there are clashes of values between young and old, and between coloureds and whites. Parents find it hard to sympathize with the repugnance of the young towards a system which, with all its faults, has given them times of relative freedom and plenty that seem like the millennium compared with the hard times they knew before. Before the world is ready to accept world citizenship as a political reality there must be a deeper understanding of the different values held by people in different communities and in different sections of society, so that a greater degree of tolerance and co-operation can be attained. It may be concluded that there is no need for pessimism, but also no time to waste, when there is so much that needs to be done in working to overcome the obstacles that lie in the way of peace.

References

1 Lorenz, K. (1963), *On Aggression*. Methuen & Co., London.
2 Tinbergen, N. (1951), *The Study of Instinct*. Oxford University Press, Oxford.
3 Hill, D. and Watterson, D. (1942), *J. Neurol. Psychiat.*, **5**, 47–72
4 Carrighar, S. (1968), In *Man and Aggression*. Edited by M. F. Ashley Montagu. Oxford University Press, Oxford, p. 37.
5 Amnesty International Annual Report 1969-70. Amnesty, Turnagain Lane, London.
6 Wilmanns, K. (1940), *Z. ges. Neurol. Psychiat.*, **170**, 583.
7 Wolff, H. G. (1960), In *Stress and Psychiatric Disorders*. Edited by J. Tanner. Blackwell, Oxford, pp. 17-33.

8 Reade, W. (1872), *The Martyrdom of Man.* Kegan Paul, Trench, Trubner & Co., London.

9 Critchley, M. (1956), *Ann. intern. Med.,* **45**, 737-747.

10 Hinkle, L. E. and Wolff, H. G. (1956), *Arch. Neurol. Psychiat.,* **76**, 115.

11 Morris, D. (1967), *The Naked Ape.* Jonathan Cape, London.

12 Boulding, K. E. (1967), In *Man and Aggression.* Edited by M. F. Ashley Montagu. Oxford University Press, Oxford, p. 83.

13 Ashley Montagu, M. F. (1968), *Man and Aggression.* Oxford University Press, Oxford.

14 Hirt, N. B. (1970), *Resolution from the Executive Body of the B.C. Section of Psychiatry,* B.C. Medical Association, West Broadway, Vancouver, B.C.

15 Neill, A. S. (1970), Personal communication.

16 *Proceedings of the International Conference on Mental Hygiene, London* (1948), Vol. IV. H. K. Lewis & Co., London: Columbia University Press, New York.

Inter-racial violence
Alan Bestic

I had my first taste of inter-racial strife in my own country, Ireland, a small, but turbulent dot on the left-hand side of Europe. The first eleven years of my life had been spent in the Irish Free State – now the Republic of Ireland – and there, as a nominal, non-church-going Protestant, I was regarded by my Roman Catholic fellow juniors as a little odd because I did not embrace what to them were the axioms of their faith. Never, however, did they attempt to proselytise, let alone harass me, despite the fact that Protestants represented less than five per cent of the population and were sitting ducks.

Then my family moved to Belfast; and once we crossed that invisible, straggling line that is the border, I found myself in a very different world, where the population of 1 500 000 was about two-thirds Protestant. Because we came from the South, the other youngsters in the neighbourhood assumed that we were 'Papists' – Catholics; and their immediate reaction bewildered me, coming as I did from an atmosphere of good humoured tolerance.

The more polite little boys asked me what school I was attending. It was not a very subtle question because education in North and South has always been segregated on religious grounds. The less polite put it bluntly: 'Are you Protestant or Catholic?' The impolite fought me first and asked questions afterwards. I was in about three skirmishes a week until I learned to run.

The fights themselves were not serious. I never got more than a minor bruise. They were, however, a sign of sickness because here were boys of my own age who had been brought up to hate Catholics and hate is not too strong a word. 'Papists' were bad. 'Prods' – Protestants – were good. Nobody told them why and it was so much a part of their lives that they never bothered to ask.

The tragedy is that in Northern Ireland today there are so many who still will not bother to ask; and, looking back over the bloodshed of the last few years, I cannot make up my mind whether I am more frightened by the violence, the irrational hate, than I am by the fact that many of the violent ones, the haters, can be reasonable and decent in every respect except that of creed. Once they enter this danger zone their minds close in the name of God and logic withers in the acid of fear.

There was a time, of course, when there was some basis for that fear. Many of those in Northern Ireland are descended from Scottish and English planters and are proud of their heritage. When a Home Rule Bill was passed by Asquith's Liberal Government in 1912 – only to be put into cold storage at the outbreak of the 1914-18 war – they were bitterly opposed to it, for to them it meant Rome Rule, a society which would be dominated by the Roman Catholic Church. They were prepared to fight rather than surrender. An Ulster Volunteer Force, which was to attract 100 000 members, was formed and arms were smuggled in, paradoxically from Germany. The Irish Rebellion of 1916 hardened the Northern resolve still further and influenced, too, the post-war British Government which in 1920 buried the Home Rule Bill and introduced instead the Government of Ireland Act which partitioned the country. Six Counties in the ancient Province of Ulster remained under the Union Jack, while the rest of the island was given dominion status.

Looking South, Northern Protestants saw literature censored by the new Government, divorce made impossible and contraceptives banned. To them that meant Rome Rule in operation, a gross interference with personal liberty; and again they prepared to defend their new sovereignty, this time legally under

44

their own Government which was responsible for all internal administration within Northern Ireland.

All police in Ulster were armed, a sight which fascinated me as a child because I had never seen a revolver before. The fact that here was the only armed police force in the British Isles meant little to me. I simply found it exciting to see men with guns in great, black, leather holsters.

These were members of the Royal Ulster Constabulary; but they were not the only armed security force. There were, also, the Ulster Special Constabulary – the 'B' Specials – an exclusively Protestant, para-military organization of part-time policemen. Their main purpose was to protect the loyal North from I R A marauders; and their presence at the time was understandable. The I R A, which opposed bitterly the treaty which gave birth to the Irish Free State and the border, was still very much alive. It was outlawed by both Northern and Southern Governments, but remained strong enough to carry out guerrilla action across the border.

As a youngster I knew little about this background of fear and less about its consequences. I was not to learn until much later that Roman Catholics in the North were treated as second-class citizens, persecuted and attacked on a scale which drove many of them to seek refuge South of the border. In the middle-class Protestant area where we lived – and Belfast to this day is segregated – nobody spoke of such matters.

I did not know that Catholics who were not in the long dole queues could get only menial jobs because the vast majority of firms were owned by the Protestant Establishment and all local or central government appointments of any worth were controlled by Protestants. I did not know that Catholics seldom got Council houses and that many lived in squalor. I did not know that few of them had the vote, simply because they were denied the privilege of being householders – or that, even if they could have gone to the polls, they could have done little to change the system for, in the arena of local government at any rate, the wards were so rigged that a Unionist majority – which, in fact, meant a Protestant majority – was elected even when there was a considerable majority of Roman Catholics in the area. I did not know of the Civil Authorities (Special Powers) Act (Northern Ireland) 1922 which gave the authorities power to imprison a person without trial for as long as they saw fit; or of the pogroms (in the name of God) in which many Catholics were killed. Northern Catholics, I must add, often were as bigoted as their Protestant opposite numbers, but at least they had the mitigating circumstances of oppression.

All those facts of life in Northern Ireland, of course, were unforgivable. They existed simply because at the time most people in the North feared a take-over which would turn orange into green, which would transform the Protestant majority into a small minority. Most Catholics were Nationalists who made it clear that they wanted unity with the South. Regrettably that fear, which lurked in every Protestant heart, was deliberately fostered by Unionist – ultra-Conservative – leaders, who knew that they would be unseated if the Protestant and Catholic working classes in this area of high unemployment were to unite and fight the Establishment at the polls. The Orange Order, a powerful influence on the Unionist Party and on most Protestants for that matter, kept memories razor-sharp. Orange parades with bands and sashes and elaborate banners acclaimed again and again the victories of the Protestant King William over the Catholic King James in the seventeenth century until they were as alive in Northern minds as the Second World War is in the minds of middle-aged men in Britain. To paint 'To Hell with the Pope' on a wall was – and is still – regarded as a patriotic duty.

This constant anti-Catholic propaganda, this inflammation of hate, was and to a considerable extent remains one of the saddest aspects of life in Northern Ireland. The flames spread indiscriminately, as I discovered just after the war, when I called with my Catholic wife on some elderly Protestant relatives in Belfast. They were gentle, kindly, old ladies and I never thought that their strict religious views would transcend family ties. Yet as soon as we entered the house the temperature sank. They tried hard to be polite, but they had never entertained a Catholic and had never wanted to do so. They wrote to my mother later: 'A nice girl. What a pity!' In all subsequent letters they referred to me as 'poor Alan', as if suddenly I had contracted an anti-social disease. Even they in their sheltered, lace-curtained lives, had been brain-washed; and as late as 1969 an unbiased study of community relations in Northern Ireland[1] by Denis Barritt, a Quaker of English parents and immense tolerance, revealed that times had not changed much. He reported: 'Protestants widely believe that Catholic priests keep their flocks in ignorance, milk them of money, while living off the fat of the land; that the Catholic Church is a monolithic body, determined to oust Protestants from the land; that the Catholic Church will never change and that any suggestion of this (e.g. the Vatican Council under Pope John XXIII) is a clever ruse to deceive naïve Protestants like the Archbishop of Canterbury. Such views do not generally penetrate in this form to the educated, professional or managerial classes, although it is often surprising how deep the prejudice is even here, many believing they are in danger of being outnumbered and that only constant and aggressive vigilance can save them.'

Yet in the years after the war the atmosphere seemed to be changing. Britain's Welfare State extended to Northern Ireland and Unionist cynics said, not without some justification: 'Not so many Catholics want to join up with the South now that they get free medical attention, better family allowances and higher dole here.'

There were, however, more telling reasons for the change in climate. In the Republic of Ireland the old-guard politicians, the veterans of the civil war with all its cancers, were dying or retiring. A new generation was more interested in a bright future than it was in the past, no matter how glorious. The power of the Roman Catholic Church, which had been considerable, was waning; and young priests were preaching radical sermons which must have shocked many an elderly bishop. The days of blind, blanket obedience were ending.

Co-operation between North and South – in hydro-electric schemes and tourism, for instance – was growing where once it would have been unthinkable; and, most significant of all, the Republican Prime Minister, Mr. Sean Lemass, and his Northern counterpart, Captain Terence O'Neill, met in Belfast in an attempt to build what Mr. Lemass described to me later as 'a climate of opinion which would allow us to look at the situation'. Never before had there been contact at such a level, and moderates on both sides of the border began talking in terms of light at the end of the tunnel. Few realized the danger of an extremist backlash. Even fewer could have guessed how violent it would become when the light went out.

Opposition to O'Neill, however, was swift after the meeting. It was personified by Dr. Ian Robert Kyle Paisley, first Moderator of the Free Presbyterian Church in Northern Ireland, a religious group which had no connexion with the Presbyterian Church, a point made very clear by both sides. Born in 1927, Dr. Paisley until the middle sixties had been more flamboyant than effective. After a disturbance at Ballymena in Northern Ireland, where the Rev. Lord Soper, a Methodist Peer, was pelted with a Bible and rosary beads, he was fined £5. When the Vatican Council opened he was in Rome to protest against Protestant Ministers 'selling out to Popery'. Soon afterwards his supporters were sticking posters on the BBC building in Belfast, accusing it of being 'The Voice of Popery'.

Only his fellow Protestant extremists took him seriously – until he began attacking Captain O'Neill for having truck with Southern Republicans. Then he caught the public mood more accurately and his thundering sermons and speeches on the 'Papist menace', delivered with the fundamentalist fervour of preachers from America's Bible belt, turned the clock back a couple of decades. Middle-aged Protestants, bewildered by change, discovered that here was a man who was saying everything that they had been taught when they were young – and he a clergyman! The lace curtains were drawn back and Paisleyism was born.

He had his silent supporters, ladies in flowered hats and white gloves, soberly clad gentlemen, who regularly attended his fiery meetings in Belfast's large Ulster Hall and dutifully put five pound notes into collection buckets. My elderly cousins would have been among them, had they been alive. Others were less silent. When he was sentenced to three months' imprisonment after a riot outside the General Assembly of the Presbyterian Church, over two thousand people gathered outside the jail. Police who tried to shift them were pelted with petrol bombs and their armoured cars were set on fire.

In that year of 1966 there were three ugly murders in Belfast. A private Protestant Army, the Ulster Volunteer Force, named after the stalwart loyalists of over forty years earlier, was formed and seemed to mirror many of Dr. Paisley's sentiments at that time, though he denied all connexion with it. Ultimately it was banned by the Northern Minister of Home Affairs under the Special Powers Act, the first time that oppressive piece of legislation had been used against a Protestant organization.

The true strength of the opposition to reform did not become apparent, however, until the autumn of 1968 and it took something quite phenomenal in Northern Ireland to reveal it. Suddenly and almost spontaneously a spirited Civil Rights movement erupted. Government leaders and Paisleyites in particular condemned it as a Republican conspiracy, but here they were wrong. Certainly there were Republicans in its ranks; but there were Socialists, Liberals, Nationalists and students, too. They marched, not under a banner of green, but one of equality; and, if the movement had substantially more Catholic supporters than Protestant, it was because most Catholics were less equal than others. Here at last was real opposition which had none of the old, inflammatory slogans about partition.

It demanded universal franchise – one man, one vote – which puzzled many people outside Ireland because always they had assumed that democracy reigned both sides of the border. They did not know that only householders or tenants of dwelling houses with rateable values of £10 or over could vote in local elections. They found it difficult to believe that constituencies could be gerrymandered. They had never heard of the ludicrous, but effective business vote. Limited companies were entitled to appoint one nominee to vote for every £10 of valuation up to a maximum of six votes; and, as most big business was in the hands of Protestants, this often meant six extra votes for the Unionists in the hands of one man.

Reform of the system by which Council houses were allocated, equality of opportunity in the labour market and the abolition of the Special Powers Act were other demands. To publicize them a committee drawn from the Derry Housing Action Committee, the Northern Ireland Civil Rights Association, the Londonderry Labour Party, the Londonderry Labour Party Young Socialists, the Derry City Republican Club and the James Connolly Society planned a protest march in Londonderry on 5 October 1968 and I feel sure that none of these bodies realized that what seemed to be a fairly routine operation was to mark the beginning of a new era.

I was in the North at the time, gathering material for a book,[2]

49

in which I wrote later: 'The Minister of Home Affairs, William Craig, banned the march through the Waterside Ward and, when the marchers reached the boundaries, they found their path was barred by police vehicles. Fighting broke out. The police drew their batons and waded into the crowd. Water cannon were turned against the demonstrators and, as the newspaper pictures revealed the following day, there were some very unsavoury scenes, one shot showing a policeman striking a young woman with his baton.

'Gerry Fitt,[3] who had been in the vanguard of the demonstrators, received a heavy blow on the head very early in the proceedings and had to have three stitches to pull the wound together. Eddie McAteer, the Nationalist leader, was hit on the shoulder. Altogether thirty people were hurt and fifteen were arrested, but what shocked most people was the manner in which the police acted.[4]

'Three British Members of Parliament, John Ryan, Russell Kerr and his wife, Ann (who was having quite a ration of riots, having just returned from Chicago[5]), were behind Fitt when he was hit; and afterwards Kerr said: "I was appalled by what I saw. Frankly I never thought to see the like of it in a part of the United Kingdom. We intend to make a report to Mr. Callaghan, the Home Secretary."

'Craig not only denied that the police had been brutal, but praised them for their action. Few observers accepted his version of the events, however, and the following day a leader writer in *The Times* wrote: "The refusal of Mr. William Craig to hold an inquiry into police methods in Londonderry cannot be the last word. His assurance that the police used no undue force echoes exactly that of Mayor Daley in Chicago last month ... This demonstration was planned to protest against gerrymandering of electoral boundaries, which few deny is widespread in Ulster and amounts to a scandal in Londonderry." '

Certainly the police emerged from this affair with little credit. Yet had television cameras not beamed it into overseas homes – including that of Mr. Harold Wilson, the British Prime Minister – the reaction might not have been so dramatic or so widespread. For perhaps the first time police violence not only took place but was seen throughout the world to take place.

50

Fresh teams of newspaper and television reporters crossed the Irish Sea. Curtains, lace and otherwise, were ripped away; and for many months to come Northern Ireland was seldom out of the news.

Those demanding civil rights welcomed the visitors. Those determined to cling to the status quo – the Protestant extremists – saw them as a threat. Followers of the Rev. Dr. Paisley became more and more active, sensing that here was a movement that could bring about the first significant change in Northern Ireland for fifty years. They were right, though they fought grimly to prevent it.

Four days after the Londonderry affair, the Derry Citizens Action Committee was formed under the chairmanship of Mr. John Hume, who had been working hard on the housing front in his native city for some time and had taken part in the march. Its sixteen members were drawn from the organizations who had been represented on 5 October and this new committee pledged itself to a strategy of non-violence.

Almost simultaneously students at Queen's University, Belfast, roused by the news from Londonderry, formed another group, People's Democracy, a founder member of which was Miss Bernadette Devlin who later became the youngest M P in the British House of Commons since Pitt. Its views were somewhat more extreme than those of, say, the Civil Rights Association, but it, too, preached non-violence and on the whole practised what it preached.

Meanwhile the telephones between No. 10 Downing Street and Stormont, seat of the Northern Parliament, were busy. On 4 November, Captain O'Neill, Mr. Craig and Mr. Brian Faulkner, Northern Ireland Minister of Commerce, were called to London by Mr. Wilson. On 5 November, the British Prime Minister told the House of Commons that he wanted an impartial enquiry into the events of 5 October and he advocated early changes in local electoral franchise. On 22 November Captain O'Neill announced that there were to be reforms: the appointment of an Ombudsman; the allocation of housing on a points system; the replacement of Londonderry Corporation by a Development Commission; the abolition of the company vote; and the eventual withdrawal of 'some Special Powers'.

The Civil Rights workers greeted the announcement with

cautious optimism. The right wing extremists, however, were even more outraged than they had been when Captain O'Neill shook hands with Mr. Lemass. The extent of their resentment – and the extent to which some police officers abused their office – is shown in the report of the impartial Commission of Inquiry which ultimately was appointed in March 1969 and which made its findings known the following August.[6]

Chairman of the three man Commission was Lord Cameron, D S C, a distinguished Scottish High Court Judge. Having outlined the events in Londonderry on 5 October, he and his colleagues reported that in the heat of the action a senior police officer had temporarily lost control of himself; that there was unauthorized use of batons and indiscriminate use of water cannon on pedestrians, together with 'unnecessary and ill-controlled force in the dispersal of demonstrators, only a minority of whom acted in a disorderly and violent manner'.

In mitigation of the police action, it stated that the demonstration was not well organized or stewarded and that there was a small element in the crowd who were prepared to provoke and initiate violence. There were, too, certain I R A members identified among the crowd and among the stewards, but, the Commissioners reported, 'there was no evidence available to the police that they intended or were likely to provoke a riot or stir up violence'.

Finally they pointed out that, if the objective of the police operation was to drive the Civil Rights movement into the ground by a display of force and firmness, it had failed. The result was the opposite, as most people outside Northern Ireland could have predicted. Those with minds locked in the strait jacket of political sectarianism cannot learn the lessons of history, however, unless they have written it themselves. Never can they understand that force cannot kill ideas or ideals; and so, when violence fails once, their only answer is to use increased violence next time around. That, at any rate, seems to have been the strategy adopted by the right wing extremists.

The Commission considered not only the events in Londonderry on 5 October, but a series of ugly disturbances which took place subsequently in various parts of Northern Ireland as the anger of those opposed to the Civil Rights campaign grew. Again it criticized not only the rioters, but the police for their partisan actions. It praised the Civil Rights workers for their discipline and it became clear to all but the Northern Ireland diehards that here was a most unsavoury situation which demanded to be changed.

The partisan attitude of the police was particularly noticeable when further trouble broke out in the Catholic Bogside area of Londonderry. A Civil Rights Association march had been banned by the Northern Home Secretary. Soon afterwards there was a spontaneous 'sit-down' protest in Shipquay Street. John Hume tried to disperse it, but a stone battle broke out when Protestant extremists gathered and soon it degenerated into a full-scale riot. For hours sporadic battles flared between police and Catholics throughout the City and Bernadette Devlin, who the previous day had been elected M P for Mid-Ulster at Westminster, wrote later of her arrival in the city: 'Derry was a battlefield. It was like coming into beleaguered Budapest; you had to negotiate the car around the piles of bricks and rubble and broken glass.'[7]

When the police withdrew under pressure, the Bogsiders sealed off their area with barricades – or partially sealed it off. They forgot two streets. That night the police returned and rampaged through the area, beating anyone they found on the street. The wise and the lucky had barricaded themselves into their houses, remembering the earlier assault; and the following day it was John Hume again who defused the situation, thereby preventing even uglier scenes. He persuaded a group of church and civic leaders to ask the Minister of Home Affairs, Captain W. J. Long,[8] to withdraw the police from the Bogside in exchange for an undertaking that peace would be preserved. The Minister accepted the proposal. The police withdrew; and for a while at any rate there was peace.

All these events were investigated by Lord Cameron and his fellow Commissioners. They found that the grievances – injustices is not too strong a word – which were thrown into such stark relief were true, and they expressed the hope that the reforms announced by Captain O'Neill would 'go a very considerable way not only to acknowledge the justice of the complaints on these points, but also the expediency and necessity of providing remedies'.

The unfortunate Captain O'Neill must have welcomed those

appreciative words from such a judicially unbiased body, for he was finding little sympathy among his own grass roots. Right wing members of his Unionist party were opposing him openly and with increasing vehemence, presumably feeling that they could impede reform by replacing him with a hard-liner.

O'Neill, however, fought back. Already he had sacked William Craig, his Minister of Home Affairs who earlier had made a speech virtually calling for a UDI, Rhodesian-style. Two months later he announced that there would be a general election on 24 February, hoping that he would win a firm mandate from the people for his reform policies.

The campaign reflected the chaos which had been spreading throughout life in Northern Ireland. There were official Unionist candidates opposed by anti-reform Unionists. There were Nationalist candidates, Northern Ireland Labour candidates, Republican Labour candidates, National Democratic candidates, Liberal, People's Progressive Party and People's Democracy candidates. The Rev. Dr. Paisley stood as a Protestant Unionist against Captain O'Neill in the Bannside constituency to which the Prime Minister had been returned unopposed throughout his parliamentary career. Bernadette Devlin opposed Major James Chichester-Clark who later succeeded Captain O'Neill.

There was little confusion, however, about the result. Two Civil Rights workers, John Hume and Ivan Cooper, a Protestant, were elected. Bernadette Devlin notched up six thousand votes against Major Chichester-Clark's nine thousand. Paisley ran the Prime Minister far too close for Captain O'Neill's comfort and the overall result did little to cheer the Prime Minister. There were a few fascinating new faces in Parliament, but no vote of confidence. Two months later O'Neill resigned.

He was succeeded by Major Chichester-Clark, and Dr. Paisley is reported to have said: 'All is well.' Certainly the extremists felt that the Major was closer to their way of thinking than the Captain, but here they misjudged the situation. The new Prime Minister under the close scrutiny of Westminster seemed determined to push through O'Neill's reform programme and soon the Paisleyites were saying: 'We got rid of a Captain. Now we'll get rid of a Major.' Their political manoeuvres among the grass roots of the Unionist Party, however, were soon overshadowed by violence on an unprecedented scale.

Anyone in Ireland – and particularly in Northern Ireland – could have seen it coming. 12 August is a day of high emotion among true-blue Protestants in Londonderry. It marks the anniversary of the famous siege in 1669, when apprentices in the City closed the gates against the forces of King James and held them at bay until relief ships reached them 105 days later. To commemorate this historic occasion about twenty thousand people march in traditional procession around the ancient walls in a display of what normally is comparatively peaceful pageantry.

The oppressive atmosphere of 1969, however, was far from normal and most sensible Protestants and Catholics knew that the procession could develop into an ugly piece of coat-trailing. They asked the Minister of Home Affairs to put a blanket ban on all processions, but this he would not do.

Those in the Bogside decided to remain in their area and ignore the procession. Taunts from the marchers, however, led to skirmishes and the police with more enthusiasm than sense launched a baton charge on the Catholic area. The local inhabitants, remembering again earlier police excesses, flung up barricades; and the battle of the Bogside was on.

Here was a phenomenon even for Northern Ireland. Half the City's population – 27 000 people – declared what amounted to Home Rule for their own area and for fifty hours they fought to maintain it, spurred on by frustration, fear and utter lack of confidence in the impartiality of the police. Bernadette Devlin was there and she has described the scene vividly and with understandable emotion in *The Price of My Soul*.

She wrote: 'We threw up barricades of rubble, pipe and paving stones – anything we could lay our hands on – to prevent the police coming straight into the area and in their own words "settling the Bogside once and for all".[9] Within the first half-hour eight police tenders were trapped in our barricades and if we'd only had the means to destroy them we would have burned those tenders out.

'It was at that point that the manufacture of petrol bombs began. The petrol bombs were made literally by pregnant women and children. Kids of seven and eight who couldn't fight made the petrol bombs and they made them pretty well. The kids of nine and ten carried them in crates to the front lines. The young girls collected stones and built barricades and the girls, the boys and the men fought on the front line against the police. The police answered our stones and petrol bombs with stones of their own and with ever increasing supplies of tear gas. The whole air was saturated with it and we had not a gas mask among us.'

While this twentieth-century siege of Derry continued, civil rights workers in ten other areas held demonstrations in an effort to divert the police who were trying to breach the Bogside barricades. One area was Belfast and there the 'B' Specials made a concentrated attack on the Catholic areas. The local people barricaded their streets, but they were no match for small arms, machine guns and armoured cars. Six people were killed, including an eight-year-old boy who was hiding with his family in a back room. Houses and factories were burned to the ground; and once more Northern Ireland made blood-thirsty headlines around the world.

Harold Jackson of *The Guardian* wrote on 16 August: 'The cartographers can start redrawing the map of Belfast now. Conway Street can be rubbed out and so can Norfolk Street. Not one house in either can ever be lived in.

'This morning a few of the shocked survivors picked over what they could find of their possessions. One young mother started, burst into tears and could only repeat time and again: "How could they? How could they?"

'This is not an impartial account for a simple reason – the Catholics who were petrol-bombed out of their homes will willingly tell their story. The Protestants who are alleged to have wreaked this primitive vengeance meet the reporter with obscenities and sticks. The authorities, who are also implicated, will say nothing.

'The two streets lie in the Falls Road area at the point where the fiercest fighting took place last night. Today the roadway is blackened and scorched, heaps of bricks lie strewn across the carriageway and the odd wisp of smoke still rises. A young man from Norfolk Street who gives his name, but would rather it wasn't used, tells what happened.

' "The police," he says, "came down at about 10 p.m., when

crowds of both religions had started to gather, to tell the Catholics that the 'B' Specials would control the Protestants. The Catholics in turn said that they would only defend themselves; if the Protestants made no move there would be no trouble.

' "About half an hour afterwards two armoured cars came down Cupar Street after the Protestants had got there and drove right at the barricades and wrecked them. Then the Protestants got through – they and the peelers were fighting hand-in-hand. A Protestant man with the peelers went along banging all the shutters in. Then the armoured car opened up and some bloke was hit on the corner by the butchers."

'The families started streaming out of their houses as the trouble grew and clustered in the area of Divis Street. Miss Bernadette Hyndman said that the "B" Specials constantly fired towards the Catholic families, making them retreat from their houses. As the police drove the families back, she said, the Protestants from Second Street and Third Street moved in behind them.

'They then started methodically burning each house in turn. Certainly it is inconceivable that the work could have been casually achieved.

'I walked along as far as it was safe – the Protestants were building a huge barricade at the end of the road and were extremely hostile – and could see that each house had been totally gutted. Many had no roof, none had any trace of furniture or fittings left inside. Even the cookers had been wrecked and the gas meters broken open. In No. 44 Conway Street water from a broken mains pipe gushed down into what had once been the kitchen.'

At last it became obvious to the Northern Ireland Government – and particularly to the British Government – that law and order was in danger of collapsing completely. To forestall that disaster British troops were moved into Londonderry, where they replaced the police. In London there must have been some anxious moments about the sort of reception they were going to be given by Catholic Republicans; but to the amazement of those outside the troubled areas, the troops were welcomed warmly by Bogside housewives, who came out from their battered houses to greet them with tea and cakes and sandwiches.

The following day more troops were sent to Belfast, but here the battle was over. Of their arrival a French journalist, Jacques Amalric, wrote in *La Monde*, a conservative daily: 'An armed British soldier stands guard on a burnt out street in a Catholic quarter. The street is right beside a Protestant quarter. At the height of the riot several fanatics had only to slip in discreetly among their neighbours and throw their Molotov cocktails to slake a century-old thirst for vengeance.

'The fire brigade was not able, or did not want to answer the call. Trapped by the fire of the snipers of the Rev. Mr. Paisley, the Catholics were helpless.

'Forty families are still taking refuge in a disused church and the blond and pink soldiers of Her Majesty patrol, submachine guns at the hip, in an atmosphere of nightmare – the last and derisory frontier of the Empire. Having arrived too late to prevent the massacre, they are protecting only ruins.'

Not only the buildings were in ruins, but community relations, too. That was clear to most observers, including members of the British Cabinet. On 19 August Major Chichester-Clark was in London, conferring with Mr. Wilson and Mr. James Callaghan, the Home Secretary. At that meeting the task of maintaining law and order in Northern Ireland was turned over to the British Army. A senior London police officer was put in charge of the Northern Ireland police and two senior British civil servants were seconded to the Northern Ireland Ministry of Home Affairs in what obviously was a watch-dog capacity. Two days later Mr Callaghan revealed that he would fly to Northern Ireland the following week for a three-day 'meet the people' tour. Four days later Baron Hunt, CBE, DSO, conqueror of Everest, was appointed Chairman of a three-man Advisory Committee 'to examine the recruitment, organization, structure and composition of the Royal Ulster Constabulary and the Ulster Special Constabulary and their respective functions and to recommend as necessary what changes are required to provide for the efficient enforcement of law and order in Northern Ireland'.

The following October the Hunt Committee presented its report[10] to the Northern Ireland Minister of Home Affairs. It recommended that the RUC should be an unarmed civilian body, similar to British police forces, and that the 'B' Specials should be replaced by a reserve force which would be under the control of the G O C, Northern Ireland, which meant, of course, that it would take its orders from London. Protestant extremists rioted in protest. Shots were exchanged between them and the British Army. The report, however, was accepted and its recommendations put into force.

July 1970, when Orange fervour was mounting, brought fresh trouble. Rumours circulated in Belfast that I R A marksmen were planning to shoot up an Orange Day parade. Strong military forces moved into streets of the Catholic area, which was put under curfew. When some youths began stoning the troops, they replied with heavy barrages of C S gas. A rigorous house-to-house search was carried out. Some arms were found, considerable damage was done and four men died, all of them civilians. The honeymoon between the Catholics and the British Army was over.

That breach in relationships which was to have such bitter, lasting results did not start a courtship between the Army and the Protestant extremists. In Londonderry one month later troops clashed with marching members of the ultra-loyalist Apprentice Boys movement. The marchers defied a ban on processions and stoned the soldiers who replied with C S gas and rubber bullets. Dr. Conor Cruise O'Brien, a Labour Member of Parliament from the Republic of Ireland, present as an observer, was attacked and injured by Protestant extremists. On 12 October the gas company near the Bogside was blown up and an empty four storey building set on fire.

That, to borrow a quiet English phrase from the cricket field, was the state of play at the beginning of 1971. But for the fact that a variety of technical problems delayed the publication of this book, it would have been the end of this chapter, apart from some wistfully optimistic thoughts of my own.

I wrote, for instance: 'The list of incidents has been long, but its length serves a purpose. It shows how violence feeds on violence, how stones are replaced by petrol bombs, petrol bombs by gelignite, gelignite by something very close to anarchy. It is remarkable that the seed of progress could gain a footing in this scorched earth. Yet most of the reforms promised by Captain O'Neill in November 1968 are being implemented.

'The Londonderry Corporation has been suspended and replaced by a Development Commission. The business vote has gone and sweeping electoral reforms are under way. The points system for housing allocation has been accepted by most local authorities. Not one, but two Ombudsmen have been appointed, the first to investigate complaints against central government departments and at Stormont, the second to operate at local government level. The R U C has been disarmed and the notorious "B" Specials have been disbanded. That last move has been particularly significant because the "Specials" had become the shock troops of oppression, the strong arm of sectarian extremism. The Special Powers Act, it is true, still exists, but it has been put into cold storage.

'There are those who argue, of course, that changes were brought about because of violence and not in spite of it. Had the flames not been seen by the world, they say, the hard-liners would have won, for it was only when police and extremist excesses were publicized internationally that the British Government intervened. There I cannot agree. The original demands were made by civil rights workers who not only practised non-violence, but often risked their own skins by trying to prevent excesses and calm those whose discipline had cracked under provocation. Had they been violent, indeed, I believe they would have been beaten, for the Establishment would have been able to explain away its actions as "firm measures to put down terrorists". In the event the violent were dwarfed by their own actions. The non-violent, so seldom dramatic, became giants.'

Those were naïve words, indeed, though reporters who over the years wrote books about the Vietnam war will sympathize with me in these circumstances. Tomorrow's napalm is yesterday's history. Between the pair of them, today gets battered beyond recognition. Within a couple of months the events of January 1971 in Northern Ireland had been relegated to the league of preliminary skirmishes. Bombings, shootings and deaths among both civilians and military became bitter daily routine, increasing in scale. Amid all the smoke, all the fire, all the blood, the moderates who had stood so tall could scarcely be seen.

Chichester-Clark was replaced as Prime Minister by Brian Faulkner. Paisley was now a Member of Parliament at both Stormont and Westminster. Two separate illegal Irish Republican Armies were waging urban guerrilla warfare, pausing only occasionally to snipe at each other over their ideological differences; and the political temperature rose to an unprecedented height.

In August the Special Powers Act that had been put into cold storage was reactivated. Internment without trial was introduced, followed immediately by a sharp increase in violence. In the two months which followed its introduction fifty-five people were killed.

To such a background, Mr. Heath, Mr. Faulkner and Mr. Jack Lynch, Prime Minister of the Republic of Ireland, met at Chequers, the traditional country home of British Prime Ministers. A year earlier this occasion would have been regarded as cause for considerable optimism. By the autumn of 1971, however, it was regarded by those close to the situation as little more than a forlorn hope for a distant future. Chequers was a million miles away from the Falls Road and the Shankhill Road in Belfast. In these areas they spoke of civil war as being inevitable.

It was argued in Britain, though on neither side of the border, that the sight of those three men around one table might give strength to the silent majority, the reasonable people who hated violence and longed only for peace. Even in better circumstances, however, silent majorities are difficult to identify, as Vice-President Spiro T. Agnew discovered in the United States of America; and the result of the only positive probe into this element in Ireland was depressing. Having made a scholarly, painstaking and exhaustive study[11] of the situation, Professor Richard Rose came to the conclusion that the moderates were a small and lonely group. Commenting upon his verdict, Harold Jackson, now a veteran of the stones and bombs and bullets, wrote in *The Guardian*: 'Here lies the heart of the Ulster problem and the element which arguably makes it unique in modern political history. What happens to the democratic tradition when a clear majority of the people persistently vote for a régime which is undemocratic in instinct? Most repressive régimes pose no problems for the liberals; they are either chosen by a privileged élite as in South Africa or are the product of undemocratic process, as in Russia.

'The dilemma in Northern Ireland which emerges plainly

from Professor Rose's study and has been evident since the issue came into prominence is that all the liberal solutions involve rigging the democratic process. This is simply the other side of the coin to a Government dedicated to law and order which suspends the process of law in an attempt to achieve order. Neither position can be maintained in logic and discussion simply bogs down in an argument about means and ends.'

Certainly Northern Ireland seems to have reached the end of one long road. As I write one third of the population and half the school-going population rejects utterly the Stormont Government machine. Only constitutional changes which will give them a voice in their own affairs will bring any form of integration.

Such changes are now under consideration; but, should they be introduced, there will be an explosion from another quarter. It seems almost inevitable that they will be rejected by rank-and-file Unionists. What, then, can prevent the outbreak of civil war, now so common a topic of conversation that it no longer sounds dramatic? As I write I can see nothing to prevent it. I can see nothing to suggest that there will not be further, far greater violence, creating a ping-pong hate which could take generations to eradicate. The people of Northern Ireland seem to be caught up in a hysteria of hopelessness. Protestants and Catholics in the battle areas have left their homes, piling their furniture on trucks and handcarts, and before they have left they have burned them to the ground in a gesture so final that it seems to border on madness. Are these people, my own people, for my mother comes from Belfast, my father from Dublin, the lemmings of Western Europe?

Seldom, indeed, can a situation have reached the point-of-no-return so quickly. Only a few months ago I wrote: 'There are, however, encouraging grounds for hope. There are men like John Hume and Ivan Cooper who never lost sight of their objectives even when they were taking personal fire brigade action to douse the flames of hysteria.

'There was the victory in the shipyards of Harland and Wolff after a battle for the hearts and the minds of the workers. "The Yard" at Queen's Island, cornerstone of Northern Ireland's economy despite Government efforts to diversify, to attract new industries, has an ugly history of sectarianism, though in recent years a revitalized trade union movement has done much to purge bitterness which could only damage the workers' cause. Violence throughout the North, however, had brought a new, dangerous tension, had resurrected old, irrational fears in "the Yard"; and, had that fear detonated the tension, had the men taken to the barricades, hopes of peace could well have died.

'It was to that background that Sandy Scott, a young, Protestant shop steward, who was Chairman of the Steel Workers' Flexibility Group, with a Protestant colleague, James McFall, a boiler-maker of the same union, took positive and courageous action. He called a meeting of all 8 000 workers; and when he was warned that he was dealing with dynamite, he said simply that they had to do something, that the situation won't go away of itself.

'He had emerged as a natural leader because of his consistent union work, but even in normal circumstances he would have been taking a risk by exposing an issue with such grim religious undertones to a public meeting. When he summoned the workers together, however, the situation was far from normal; and on the eve of the meeting, on the night of 14 August, it was catastrophic for all hell had broken loose in Belfast.

Nevertheless, he carried on. He held his meeting, while workers throughout Northern Ireland watched from a distance, awaiting the result, awaiting a lead. He proposed a resolution, calling for peace, stressing that violence could lead only to economic disaster and demanding stronger government measures to prevent civil disorders. It was passed unanimously and had a profound affect not only on Queen's Island, but on every worker – and every employer – in Northern Ireland.

'It did not complete Sandy Scott's immediate task, however. Because of the previous night's violence, many Catholic workers had stayed at home. They felt their families were in danger and were not too sure, either, of the way in which their Protestant fellow-workers would greet them. That night Sandy Scott, James McFall and others climbed the barricades at the Falls Road and told the Catholics that it was safe to come back. The following night they joined the vigilante peace groups, which were operating in the danger spots and which were made up of men of both religions.

63

'Later Sandy Scott was awarded an MBE – which he omitted to mention to me, incidentally, when I met him – but it was not simply for his actions on those few explosive days and nights. It was for his long-term work for peace in an area that was becoming dangerously inflamed.

'Men like Scott bring to Northern Ireland a glimmer of hope. So do inter-denominational organizations such as PACE, which spells out the initial letters of Protestant and Catholic Encounter as well as a message of peace. It was founded in 1969 by a group of Catholics and Protestants who felt a need to meet together, to learn as much as they could about each other and to discuss freely their points of agreement and disagreement. The Management Committee consists of joint Catholic and Protestant Chairmen, a Secretary and a Treasurer and four other members, two Catholic and two Protestant.

'Local groups are being formed throughout Northern Ireland by what the Management Committee describes as "men of known goodwill who desire to create a community in which social justice and social charity are the cornerstones". Already it has met Dr. R. Simpson, MP, who heads the newly formed Ministry of Community Relations, which has close relations with the Community Relations Commission, from which it has received a grant of £1 000 and has founded ancillary organizations for women and young people – the Young PACE Association and Women Together. Young PACE is for those between the vital ages of 14 and 25 years; and Women Together was formed to make "full use of the great influence for peace which women can have in their family and community".

'The importance of women in a troubled community was put to me very simply in Belfast by Mrs. Monica Patterson, a member of the PACE Secretariat. She is, as she says herself, "a militant Catholic", who lived most of her life in London; and she told me: "A community, remember, is made up of homes and families. A lot of people have lost pride even in their streets; and so the first thing we tell women is just how important it is to keep the streets swept.

' "We want to offer these women interests outside the home. I have a group engaged in what we call the Albert Bridge scheme. In the past few weeks they have organized knitting demonstrations, visits to the Planetarium and so on. It is a mixed group that includes working-class women from the troubled areas as well as middle-class professional women."

'Knitting demonstrations and flights of fancy to the stars may seem insipid vaccines with which to fight the virus of bigotry. Yet they are working, perhaps because they seem so innocuous. They are bringing together women who might never have spoken to each other because of class and creed; and two happenings at the height of street battles have proved what an important part women can play in the cause of peace.

'On July 1970 troops were being stoned by gangs of youths in the predominantly Catholic area of Ballymurphy, Belfast. With growing frustration the women watched this senseless violence. Then about thirty of them walked into no-man's land between the two forces; and the battle was over.

'One of them, Mrs. Mary Grogan, said later: "We were just disgusted, browned off with all the trouble. We've had too much of it. Our own young people were playing football and a crowd of youngsters came up to the corner and started throwing stones at the military.

' "About thirty of us women went out and stood across the road. There were also some young men nearby just in case we needed them. We gave the youngsters a good talking to and then they went off."

'Another housewife, Mrs. Theresa Donnelly, said that the secret of their success was the fact that they were women. "They take more heed of us than they do of men," she added. "We can do better than the men. We have more guts than the men."

'The following night there was a powder-keg situation in the predominantly Protestant Shankill Road area of Belfast. A crowd of about 500 began moving up Snugville Street towards an Army command post. About a hundred women moved into the road to form a human barricade and told men of the Second Battalion, Parachute Regiment, to stand back. Then they lectured the marchers and told them to go home. After some foot shuffling, they did so.

'Later Mrs. Doris Swan said: "All the women were worn out, but it was a job that had to be done. We went down because we felt we could do more than the men and, if trouble breaks out again, we will go down again and see what we can do."

'The action of these women could be an example, not only to Northern Ireland, but to other parts of the world. Surely they must have been welcomed by John Hume, who wrote in *The Sunday Press* on 18 October 1970: "What price is one prepared to pay to achieve one's objectives? Violence is uncontrollable. When the first stone is thrown, one never knows where it will end or what destruction to human life or property may take place...

' "It is easy to throw a stone or to preach hatred. It is much more difficult to be constructive, to control one's emotions and to try to find a way forward. Violence will never find a way, and those who promote it on either side might examine their consciences and recall the words of Gandhi: 'Wars are declared in the name of humanity, but they are created by human ambition.' " '

I met John Hume shortly after he had written those words. He spoke then with a quiet, disciplined optimism. I doubt, however, whether he or Sandy Scott, the idealists of PACE or those brave, sane women from Ballymurphy and the Shankill Road could have envisaged the savagery which lay ahead of them. I hope that they all retain some vestige of optimism, but I cannot see how that could be possible. The men and women who fostered bigotry so coldly and so skilfully over the decades to protect their privileges are the only victors at the moment. The damage that they have done and are doing, I fear, will not be repaired by this generation.

As I write the Northern Ireland Parliament at Stormont has been suspended and power transferred to the British Government in an attempt to curb death and destruction caused by mounting I R A action. At best the move is a gamble with comparative peace the prize. Should it fail, there will be increased violence. Either way, the scars will remain for a long time. Tragically over the years they have been reopened too easily and too often.

References

1 *Orange and Green*, published by the Northern Friends Peace Board, Brigflatts, Sedbergh, Yorkshire (3s. 6d.).
2 *The Importance of Being Irish*, Cassell and Co., London

(35s.); William Morrow and Co., Inc., New York ($5.95).

3 Labour M P at both Stormont and Westminster, to which Northern Ireland returns twelve members.

4 I was wrong. The final count showed that seventy-seven civilians and eleven policemen were injured.

5 She had been there for the Democratic Convention at which local police did little to enhance their reputation by the fashion in which they curbed demonstrators.

6 *Disturbances in Northern Ireland*, Her Majesty's Stationery Office (10s.).

7 *The Price of My Soul*, by Bernadette Devlin, Alfred Knopf, New York ($5.95).

8 He succeeded William Craig, sacked by Captain O'Neill on 11 December 1968.

9 A phrase one police officer used to Mary Holland of *The Observer*. He added: 'If we don't, we're done for!'

10 'Report of the Advisory Committee on Police in Northern Ireland', Her Majesty's Stationery Office (5s.).

11 *Governing without Consenters*, Faber and Faber (£6).

Students in revolt
William G Burrows

In any consideration of the subject of violence in the US, one
must not lose sight of the fact that this is a country founded on
revolution; and it has become a country in which violence, for
one reason or another, has become part of the accepted way of
life. Americans are proud of the revolution which launched
their young republic on its epic journey from colonial status
to that of major world power. In the centuries which have intervened, however, while that revolution became sanctified, any
other revolutionary activity has become increasingly abhorrent
to the Establishment.

The history of student unrest in the United States is now
well known. Of the major historical factors influencing our
progress to the present state of affairs, the first of these is
certainly racism. The concept of first and second class citizens has dictated that first of all American Indians, then
American blacks, then Americans of Mexican descent, and
finally Americans of Puerto Rican background must be treated
as though somehow inferior to the all-white citizens. In many
areas they have been herded into ghettos of substandard living
accommodation; deprived of equal rights of citizenship, education, and occupation. For many decades, the second class citizens accepted their lot with little complaint. The situation today
is different.

Another factor in student unrest was the development of a small group of young citizens, the Flower Children or Hippies, who decided to opt out of the materialistic culture of modern America. Idealistic and altruistic, these young people really believed that in the midst of a culture of materialism, acquisition, and total emphasis on financial success, they could live a life based on love of one another and respect for all aspects of human life. Anyone familiar with the Haight-Ashbury district of San Francisco in the early 1960s could not help but be touched by the genuineness and a certain naïve purity which they projected. They were despised and hated by many because they were 'different'; considered dirty and shiftless and un-patriotic – in short, un-American.[1] It is unfortunate that their movement was ultimately doomed to failure, since its members sought to live as well-intentioned and loving parasites on the very system they hoped to alter and eventually replace. The Haight-Ashbury is a different place now. The Flower Children have gone, replaced by drug abusers and burned-out alcoholics, by pimps and prostitutes and drug pushers. It has become a place of crime, and has joined the long list of areas in American cities where it is unsafe for people to be about at night.

Probably the first warning of what lay ahead was the formation of the organization 'Students for a Democratic Society', (S D S), which issued its manifesto and made its first demonstration in 1962. In 1968 a splinter group, the so-called Yippies ('Youth Independent Party'), sought to disrupt the Democratic National Convention in Chicago, and succeeded in arousing the wrath of a police force, which appeared to many to have been waiting eagerly to be provoked. To be fair, it must be admitted that the provocation offered by the Yippies was extreme, and their behaviour generally was not calculated to attract public sympathy towards their cause. But if publicity was their major goal, they certainly achieved it.

By this time, riots were developing on various college and university campuses with almost monotonous regularity; a complete recitation of all the institutions involved would be redundant, but several highlights stand out. The University of California at Berkeley became a battleground in 1968. It was at the State College in San Francisco that this author first experienced a student 'strike'. In those days, my teaching duties involved me in a trip by car along a route past the State College. After two occasions of finding myself stopped, my car surrounded, jostled, and almost overturned by turbulent, brawling groups of student demonstrators and police, I soon adopted a different route. It was at San Francisco State that one saw the development of a specially-trained police force brought into being specifically to deal with student agitators, the so-called 'Tactical Squad' or 'Tac Squad'. This group, sometimes referred to as America's first storm-troopers, must have been a fearsome sight to the student agitator. All large, burly men, they were outfitted in special body armour, including thick plexi-glass helmets; they were armed with five-feet plastic batons, tear gas, mace aerosols, and (for a last resort use) hand guns and shotguns. They went about their business with chilling efficiency. At Berkeley, during the unfortunate episode of the People's Park, a police helicopter sprayed the demonstrating crowd below with tear gas, only to have the wind carry it into the open windows of a nearby hospital. (It should be explained that the People's Park was a small plot of unused, city-owned land in Berkeley which had been quietly cleaned up, landscaped and planted as a park by a group of local residents. The city authorities decided it should become a parking-lot, tore up the flowers and shrubs, erected a fence and prepared to build the parking-lot. The local residents, proud of what they had developed, reacted hotly, and skirmishes with patrolling police soon grew into riot proportions.) In Montreal, student agitators succeeded in destroying by fire the computer centre of a small university, causing a five million dollar loss to the faculty. (As a Canadian myself, it is only fair for me to point out that this event was a shattering blow to Canadian smugness, for the average Canadian, no doubt over-reacting to fears of being influenced and taken over by his huge neighbour to the south, has always considered himself an instant expert on all American problems. And the discovery that Canadian universities were not immune to the rising tide of unrest had a sobering effect on many outspoken self-appointed experts north of the border.)

During this past summer one must refer, with a sense of shame, to the tragedy of Kent State University where National guardsmen shot and killed four students, and to the University of Wisconsin where more life and property were destroyed by a bomb. During this period, several black students were shot by police during a riot at Jackson State College, a black college in the south-east. The Kent State and Wisconsin killings created a lengthy furore in the national news media; the murder of several blacks caused scarcely a ripple in comparison. The list of such episodes is tragically long; the developmental process, the escalation from protest to property damage to murder, is distressingly similar when viewed from a 'natural history' point of view.

When one studies the manifestations of student unrest, one finds that in nearly every case the process of escalation is as similar, as predictable as the choreography of a ballet. To begin with, the students banding together in groups, begin to complain about what they feel are the wrongs of society generally, or the university in particular. In many cases, they are aided and abetted, either tacitly or openly, by junior faculty who support them and perhaps gain vicarious satisfaction through egging them on.[2] There is a similarity, indeed a uniformity about the students' complaints. They complain about the outmoded, materialistic, work-oriented culture of the United States, with its emphasis on things instead of people, and its toleration of islands of terrible poverty and despair in the midst of the world's greatest affluence. They inveigh against American participation in war, particularly the Vietnam war, in which they see American intervention as unnecessary, immoral, and entirely political and cynical in its motives.[3] Attempts to arouse their enthusiasm by appeals to patriotism or national security are met with ridicule. They point quite rightly to the iniquities of the racist system of the United States, and the pathetically few gains which have been made as a result of civil rights legislation. They demand 'Black Studies departments' at their universities or colleges, usually without specific ideas about what such departments should teach, except to serve as a means of upgrading the status of the black citizen by increasing his self respect. They point to the lack of relevance of their education, not just to the lives that they will live if the present system continues, but particularly to the sort of life they hope to bring about under a new system. And finally, they have recently begun to complain about the pollution of man's environment by man. They are increasingly infuriated by the lack of needed action on the part of politicians, and the cynicism by which legislative

71

action to produce cleaner air and water is successfully blocked by the wealthy lobbies of the various industries causing the pollution. (Lobbying, in United States' political life, is not only legal, but a force to be reckoned with.) They are concerned with what they see as the idiocy of a system in which prosperity and affluence are geared to a constant semi-war footing, where already well-qualified young engineers in the aerospace and electronic industries are losing their jobs, and this year's young graduates are unable to find work. When they hear from the government spokesmen that 1·7 million defence jobs will be terminated before the end of the fiscal year 1970-71 'in the process of de-escalating the war in Vietnam', they ask, quite rightly, what this means in terms of their own future economic security.

Their first efforts to bring about change take the form of peaceful demonstrations, parades, the carrying of banners and signs, and speeches made over public address systems; again, in these efforts they are frequently urged on or advised by junior faculty members not yet fully indoctrinated in the American dream as seen from the Establishment point of view. When these efforts produce no effect, the next stage of development is the 'strike' or confrontation, with the goal of shutting down the university or college until their demands have been met or negotiated upon. Such confrontations are characterized by a great deal of strident shouting or obscenities on the part of the students; by a total disregard of such democratic process as exists to bring their complaints to the attention of the institution's administration; and by continuous rounds of meetings on one topic or another which seem to prevent participants getting any rest at all, and which are reminiscent of Pavlov's 'stage of paradoxical excitement'.[4] The next stage is the escalation of the strike into actual property damage; the students have come to believe that the administration will not listen to them until some glass is broken or a building occupied or set on fire. When property damage does not succeed in bringing about the attention sought, the next stage is physical violence. On the part of the students, this means anything from throwing bricks, attacks with sticks against anyone who opposes them, even sometimes experimenting with amateur bombs. Inevitably, violence on the part of the students is met with greater violence on the part of the authorities. Universities and colleges are not

72

equipped to police themselves when faced with mobs and riots, and almost invariably outside law enforcement agencies are called in.[4] These forces – police, Highway Patrol, National Guard – in turn, react with excessive violence to the provocation of the students, with frequently tragic results. The students are quick to point out that no policeman called into a university campus has ever been killed. The process erupts from time to time, and place to place across this great land, as one institution after another ignites as a flash point. It is not being overly-histrionic to record that many realistic, conservative observers, better informed than I as students of the American scene, are now privately maintaining that the systematic spread of campus violence and killing across the country represents the beginning of the second American revolution. Some of the more violent radical groups have announced that the second American civil war has already started. But it is a proven fact that in many parts of the country, particularly in the major cities, guerrilla warfare is being waged with police forces as the enemy, the targets of snipers and bombers. Last year eighty-six police were murdered in line of duty in such situations; for the first ten months of this year the number is sixty-seven.

One may ask what sort of students are involved in these distressing activities, and it is possible to isolate and describe at least seven well-circumscribed groups.[5] First are the *political activists*, the leaders, the hard core who plan and initiate and direct the revolt. It must be noted that radical activism cuts across the major party lines and platforms; Democrat or Republican means nothing to these young people. They tend to come from a middle class or upper-middle class family background, frequently professional, and to be of better than average intelligence. Educationally they tend to be enrolled in such studies as sociology, law, or the arts; rarely are the radical activists drawn from a medical, business, or scientific course. The next group is the large silent majority of *passive protestors*; the ones who cannot initiate action for themselves but who can easily be motivated by the activist leaders and follow along like sheep to demonstrate and riot and destroy, on order, when the process of rioting has begun.

A third group encountered are the *ex-students* – the dropouts – young people who, for a variety of reasons, have opted out of the educational system but who still hang on the fringes of their university or college, and whose discontent is readily mobilized when protestors and rioters are needed. Another identifiable group are the *racists*, and other minority groups who, while having their own political axe to grind, will attempt to use student discontent and rioting to bring about specific changes they wish for their own particular group. And finally there are the *non-students*, the young people who have never been students in a university or college but who are, for a variety of reasons, involved actively in the rioting process. These are the individuals about whom the nation's law enforcement authorities are beginning to ask questions, for it has been noted that not infrequently the same individuals turn up at one university riot after another, moving on, or out of sight, when the turmoil is finally over.

Another discrete but usually small group is a quiet *conservative minority* who simply want to get an education to fit themselves for an adult career; they are more concerned with this than with trying to alter the type of world they will have their career in. It is not uncommon to find such students moving from one strike-torn university to another less-troubled one in order to escape the turmoil and simply get on with their educational plans.

Finally – although they are not usually involved in student protest – one new group of students currently coming to the attention of student health services in universities and colleges should be mentioned, the so-called '*alienated*' students.[6] Psychiatrists and student health services are inclined to look upon this problem as a new syndrome, developing, as it usually does, in students of previously good personality. Students suffering from 'alienation syndrome' tend to live completely in the present, uncommitted to people or ideas; they have little or no communication with adults, either at home or in school, and avoid attempts on the part of adults to establish such communication. They tend to be promiscuous, leading a shallow but active sex life, moving rapidly from partner to partner, unable to make any deep relationships. They have ill-defined self-concepts and are subject to fits of sudden and intense depression, frequently leading to suicide. Usually unable to study or concentrate, it is this complaint which frequently brings them to the attention of the student health service. These are the students on college and university campuses who are involved in drug abuse and experimentation. Drug abuse, as such, seems to play little, if any, part in student revolt and unrest.

To carry out the aims of the various groups of activists involved, it is only to be expected that formal organizations should spring up, and such has indeed been the case. Mention has already been made of the Students for a Democratic Society. At about the same time as this group was being formed, similar semi-anarchistic organizations, calling themselves 'The New Left' and 'The Third World' came into existence. It is in the natural history of movements and organizations for splinter groups to break off from the original parent body, and this has, of course, been the case in the original activist organizations. One hears little nowadays of the Students for a Democratic Society; presumably its more active members have gone underground, or left the country. But a splinter group from the S D S, calling itself the 'Weathermen', would appear, at the present time, to be the most violent of the activist associations at work on university campuses.

On the racist front, the Black Panthers have become a force to be reckoned with in some areas of the country. Originally developing as a semi-military organization, they have, in some places, been suppressed and have changed their name, for example, in the midwest to 'The Society to Combat Fascism'. In other parts of the country, they are attempting to change their image and are engaging in social work, such as providing hot breakfasts for black children in poverty areas. Meanwhile, several of their outlawed leaders have succeeded in fleeing the country, and are living in Africa, Cuba, and North Korea, while still attempting to fan the flames of racism in the U S.

Not to be outdone, the American Indian, having almost committed suicide (with the able assistance, if not the outright planning, of the white sector of society), has begun to make his voice felt as well. A 'Red Power' movement has come into being as a counterpart to the 'Black Power' of the American Negro. It is of interest to note that whereas blacks who collaborate with the white Establishment are known in the Black Power movement as 'Uncle Toms', American Indians who collaborate with the white Establishment are known by their Indian peers as 'Uncle Tomahawks'; suggesting a sense of humour which one had not previously expected in these unfortunate people.

Much has been speculated and argued about the role of violence in society; some astute observers have postulated that the violence in our society comes from attempted adaptation to too rapid environmental change.[7] Mankind has always been subject to environmental change, and the story of human existence is one of constant adaptation to meet change. But within the last fifty years, with the explosion of knowledge and technology, it would seem as though environmental change is occurring too rapidly for mankind to assimilate it; violence is seen as a response to the breakdown of the adaptation process.

It is appropriate for us to ask what factors may be contributing to this process of violence, and I hasten to add that the list which follows must be viewed as incomplete, speculative, and unproven. With this reservation I would suggest that any such listing of factors must begin with the undoubted reality of human aggression as part of man's personality structure. Whether one subscribes to the biological instinctual theory,[8] or the frustration theory,[9] or the social learning theory[10] as the cause of human aggression, it must be accepted that aggression is part of man's essential life; indeed, without it our species would probably not have developed to its present stage of biological dominance. Another factor which some authorities point to is the very normal and essential stage of adolescent rebellion, which every healthy adolescent must grow through on the rocky road to maturity.[11] Undoubtedly, in our affluent society in which parents tend to give more things to their children than they give to themselves, the adolescent's ambivalent feelings are intensified and no doubt worked through in many campus rebellions. Another theory maintains that permissiveness has laid the foundation for youthful activism; that young people brought up under the doctrines of Dr. Spock can only be expected to reject authority later on. Unfortunately, this theory does not hold water, for such methods of child rearing have been subjected to continuing studies for many years, revealing that permissiveness 'creates a democratic rather than an authoritarian attitude'. It has been suggested that student activists express publicly the concerns their parents hold privately. From such studies one may postulate that the conflict that we see today may be in part between adults of middle America (the silent majority) and the adults who hold opposite socio-political attitudes (the silent minority) and whose children are the activists, the vocal minority.[12]

Some have suggested – and perhaps not too cynically – that American history itself must be taken into consideration when we talk about violence in this country, for they point out that the original settlers were people who were maladapted to the prevailing situations in their home countries and who journeyed to the United States because of their inability to adapt. The US, they say, has been settled by drop-outs and psychopaths, and if we can believe anything of the history of some of the colourful figures of the early West, one is tempted to subscribe to such a theory. If this is so, one may validly ask what has such a predominance of this type of person done to the national genetic pool over the decades?

Perhaps another factor contributing to the discontent of today is that America no longer has a frontier. For many years this was a frontier country; there was always something on the other side of the hill, an untamed land to be settled, wild beasts to be killed or domesticated, Indians to be fought, forests to be cut down and fields to be ploughed out of the wilderness, homes and towns to be built; but now civilization has spread to the Pacific seaboard. Indeed, the overcrowding there suggests a lemming-like rush to the sea; perhaps it is not accidental that California has the highest suicide rate, the highest rate of alcoholism and drug abuse in the country. And in the underpopulated states, where there is still something of a frontier condition, such social problems are not so apparent. Perhaps the lack of a challenge in the form of a frontier contributes in some part to American violence.

Reference has already been made to the unfortunate tendency towards racism, and I have no wish to belabour this point. One wonders whether racist ideas can ever be legislated out of existence, and how many decades or centuries it will take for human beings everywhere to ignore the colour of a man's skin in forming their relationships with him. I can only quote from a personal experience of a friend and colleague who happens to be black, a man well trained in both psychiatry and in public health, who not long ago was commissioned by his university to carry out a rather delicate piece of negotiation. In the course of this, he had to call upon a senior white academician with whom he had a most cordial and productive interview, at the end of which his host escorted him to the door and, in the course of saying good-bye, remarked quite casually and – my friend feels more from conditioning than from either overt or covert hostility – 'You know, I didn't realize they were letting niggers do this sort of work now.'

Perhaps another factor which should not be overlooked is the clause in the American Constitution which gives the American citizen the right to bear arms. Undoubtedly, when the Constitution was drawn up, there was good reason for this, and the early citizen needed fire arms for protection. (In some parts of the U S, from its capital city on down, this situation would still seem to exist.) But perhaps the total picture has altered to such an extent that the citizen doesn't really need to bear arms; perhaps the free right for every American to bear arms may now contribute more damage than the supporters of the Constitution in its entirety would like to admit. In any event, in spite of the assassinations of President Kennedy, Senator Kennedy, and Martin Luther King, in spite of a moving plea by President Johnson at that devastating, humiliating time for adequate gun-control legislation, in spite of the fact that all public opinion polls after the last assassination showed that more than two-thirds of the entire population wanted adequate gun controls, these gun controls have not yet been passed by Congress. It has been alleged that the National Rifle Association, a group of manufacturers of fire arms and ammunition, has succeeded in preventing, by means of lobbying, the development of adequate gun control legislation;[13] certainly the members of the N R A are vociferous in demanding their right to own and use hand guns as well as rifles and shotguns. This is a country of slogans and bumper stickers; one has become accustomed to one of the latter which reads, 'When guns are outlawed only outlaws will have guns'.

Another fact which may perhaps have some bearing on the eruption of violence, particularly in the major cities, is that of overcrowding.[14] When one considers the work of the British psychologists, Russell and Russell, utilizing caged rats which were allowed to reproduce unhindered in an environment of fixed size, it might not be too surprising that human beings crowded into inadequate housing and filthy tenements may also turn on each other in blind rage and destruction.[15] The so-called 'overload theory' has been described, as well, as contributing to dehumanization, a characteristic which seems to have become an accepted part of life in some of the larger American cities, where a human being may die in the street and be stepped over by other passers-by who simply 'don't want to get involved'.[16] Educators have pointed out that United States' youth are, until they reach college age, amongst the most coerced people on earth.[17] It is customary to think of American youth as spoiled by their parents, coddled by their teachers, dominating the P T A who in turn browbeat the teachers, and in fact generally ruling the roost. In point of fact, the demands upon American school children and teenagers to conform, to be popular, to learn to earn – the inevitable 'paper-route'! to take part in a myriad of school activities, keeps them subjected to almost constant pressure. Society provides no time to sit and think, or talk; such activity is frowned on as 'goofing off'. In any news-paper or periodical, the description of any 'good citizen' in-cludes invariably such a statement as 'He (or she) arranges his busy schedule to include' – and here follows an exhausting list of activities, all of which go to make up 'good citizenship'. Leisure, for both children and their parents, is unknown as such; when it exists, it must be planned for and worked at. The American child is early indoctrinated into the importance of business for the sake of being busy. It has been said by some European cynics that this is part of the American Puritan ethic; and that the American male is kept much too busy to have a mistress; he couldn't work her into his 'busy schedule'. (And if he could afford the time, he would certainly be much too tired to do much about it.) Yet when the regimented child finally reaches college where he is given some choice in how his time will be spent, the sudden loss of pressure must be well nigh overwhelming.

Anyone who watches American television must develop some feelings about the role of violence on television as a condition-ing technique for the young.[18] Much has been speculated about this, and some good research has been done suggesting that an acceptance of violence can be conditioned early into children.[10, 21] Be that as it may, most American schoolchildren spend more time watching television during their school years than they do attending school;[19] the average child, it has been estimated, has, by the time he finished high school, spent at least 15 000 hours sitting in front of a TV set.[20] The leaders of the television industry and the large corporations which utilize television as an advertizing medium are loud in assuring us that television cannot affect behaviour; at the same time, they completely undermine the validity of such claims by the fact that they utilize this medium for one reason alone, namely that it does affect behaviour – buying behaviour.

It has been suggested that one potential reason for the terrible gap which exists between the young and their parents today is that in colleges and universities young students have no 'father figures' upon which to model themselves.[22] It would be fair to point out that in the average American family, the American child, particularly the male, has very little contact on a personal level with his father. The American dream says 'I want my children to have all the things I didn't have'; we therefore find fathers holding two jobs in order to earn the necessary money to buy these things. It becomes easier to give the child five dollars to 'get him out of your hair' than to spend some time with him. It has been demonstrated that the mental mechanism of identification is of great importance in learning; it is known that students tend to select role-models during university and college careers, but in the average American college or university, climbing the academic ladder takes one away from students. Professors become grantsmen, writers, researchers, and travellers. Teaching – actual teaching of students – is all too frequently done by young graduate students scarcely older or more mature than the students they teach. It has been said and not without some truth, that if a student in the US wants to talk with his professor, he must ride out to the airport with him.

Another factor which must be mentioned as a possible contributor is simple boredom. The primary educational system in many schools in the United States does not challenge the students; in many instances, it has been more concerned with making United States citizens out of a group of immigrant children than in engaging their intellectual attention. I suspect that this carries over into some colleges and universities as well. If the student's attention cannot be caught, he will either stay in school, learning nothing but drifting with the tide, or else, from sheer boredom, will drop out, in either case becoming a ready prey for any type of excitement, socially acceptable or otherwise. A factor which must be considered in conjunction with boredom is the ability or lack of ability to obtain not only gainful, but meaningful employment. Most people would agree that in our culture man needs meaningful work as part of his system of self-respect, of ego satisfaction; indeed, in the US culture, with its emphasis on work and busyness, this is particularly true. What a blow it must be, therefore, for a young person to find no means of obtaining gainful employment. For the members of minority groups, in which one finds the highest unemployment rates in the country, violence may be indeed one answer, one way of striking back at a society which deprives them of a means of obtaining a little self-respect.

Yet another factor which undoubtedly plays some role in the total picture is the fact that war, or war-like events such as riots, are not without excitement, pleasure, and camaraderie, the human animal being the perverse and illogical creature that it is. Admittedly, hand in hand with such emotions go pain, distress, bereavement, suffering, fear, and boredom; but somehow these can be overlooked, especially in a major war. Perhaps it is something to do with the male's need to 'prove' himself; I suspect that this attitude is greater amongst males than females, though I have heard occasional women look back with a sense of nostalgia to wartime experiences. Certainly, many who lived in Britain during the worst days of the blitz describe the excitement, the friendship, the co-operation, the sense of closeness, 'all in it together'; they tell about how the traditional British class system, with its inherent shyness and seclusiveness broke down and people treated each other like human beings regardless of status, and of how all this reverted back to normal when the war was over. One often senses a sort of nostalgia for the 'good old days'.

Another potential factor in the overall problem which, on initial consideration, may sound rather far-fetched but which might, in point of fact, occasionally play a contributing role, has been suggested by researchers in Southern California who, in the course of routine blood examinations, discovered a large percentage of the population they were testing to be suffering from sub-clinical lead poisoning as a result of the tetraethyl lead used as an additive in petrol.[25] This has led to some surmise that perhaps occasional acts of unplanned, spontaneous, mindless violence which one encounters from time to time, especially in crowded, smoggy U S cities, might result from the toxic effects of lead.

While student revolt, up until now, has cut across the traditional party lines and political affiliations, one cannot entirely disregard as fantasy the possibility that ideological factors may be contributing to the total scene. It is, of course, common for Europeans to laugh at Americans as being 'paranoid about Communism', and 'seeing Communists under every bed', and undoubtedly, Communism is a tender subject in the US, a word which produces almost as much affect in most areas of American society as the term 'socialized medicine' does at a meeting of the American Medical Association. However, law enforcement authorities are beginning to wonder who is training and financing the non-students who appear at riot after riot. It is also a documented fact that Canadian students who are members of the outlawed group 'Federation for a Free Quebec', have boasted that some of their members have been trained in guerrilla warfare in Jordan and Cuba. Without wishing to subscribe to a paranoid theory, one might suggest that if any country hostile to the aims and ambitions of the US wished to subvert this country, or to belittle it somewhat in the eyes of the rest of the world, it might be well worth while investing a little money in the more anarchistic element of the student activists.

But for this observer, two factors stand out as the major contributions to the present situation. Undoubtedly amongst the frustrated young especially of ethnic minorities, violence must be allied to the terrible sense of hopelessness, despair and impotence which develops when, time after time, all efforts to bring about some change in the American system by democratic process come to naught. Once one has given up all hope of producing change through peaceful methods, the temptation to resort to other alternatives is an understandable one. And behind this student despair and hopelessness lies, in my opinion, the major cause of the entire situation, namely, a clash of cultures.[22] The old American Dream, the Horatio Alger story, stressed the virtues of hard work, thrift, self-denial, puritanism, looking out for oneself, acquisition, the 'rags to riches' story held out as the ideal to American youth at the beginning of this century. The end result reached is a culture in which human values are shelved in favour of acquisition and power, self-centredness, two cars in every garage, life-long commitment to hire-purchase in order to reach the 'American standard of living'; the giving of things or money to one's children as a substitute for giving one's self; the toleration of terrible poverty amidst great wealth in the most affluent society on earth; a medical system, dominated by what many Americans see as a group of greedy, rich, self-centred medical businessmen, where only the well-to-do can afford adequate medical care, a nation devoted to 'consumerism' in an ever increasing spiral of earning and spending. And all of this strange cornucopia is balanced on a military-minded complex, depending on a semi-war footing to maintain present levels of 'prosperity'. Were the East Asian war to end tomorrow, this country would be plunged into a depression the likes of which the world has never seen before.

Yet, to give a balanced picture, one must not listen only to the critics of American society, within and without her boundaries. In fairness, it must be pointed out that no nation in history has ever given so much of its wealth and expertise in foreign aid, to help developing nations, to repair war damage, to aid the victims of natural disasters. Cynics may say that foreign aid is not without its political 'strings', but the fact remains that the American taxpayers foot the bill. Americans may justifiably point with pride to their numerous civilian medical and technical missions, where altruism brings no monetary gain. The fact remains that through that strange dichotomy which exists between individual and group dynamics, the individual American, caught up in the old materialistic culture, remains one of the most kindly and generous human beings the human race has produced.

Some Americans say that the American dream has become the nightmare of a frightened and disillusioned society; but now from the furore and confusion a new American culture is developing, a culture feared and resisted by the defenders of the *status quo*, the culture of the young. This is a culture which says 'People are more important than money, ideas more important than things; human love should count for something; war and those who thrive by it are immoral; no one should be penalized because of his skin pigment; medical care should be available to all; big business interests should not be allowed to destroy the atmosphere we live in, the amenities of this small, overcrowded globe.'

Idealistic? Impractical? Stupid? Perhaps as a system it wouldn't work, given the imperfection of the human character? In any event, more and more of our young are rejecting the value systems of the parent generation and thinking along such lines. We think that we have trouble nowadays with students in colleges and universities; current studies indicate that the children coming along in high schools are even more radical in their thinking, and in a very short time they will be swelling the numbers of the 'college radicals'. Far from abating, the conflict will be enlarged, and fanned and extended, fanned and encouraged, no doubt, by new radical groups with their own personal axes to grind.

For the native-born American not blinded by his country's official propaganda (the best, incidentally, in the world in this observer's experience), the present situation is distressing, confusing, and very divisive. For those who have come as aliens to live in the US, simply because they love this country and their American friends and colleagues, the impact is little less than devastating.

And what, so far, has been the result of all this strife and struggle and distress? One may sum it up by describing the present development of what seems to be a conservative backlash. So far the result of student strikes, demonstrations, and violence has usually taken the form of more laws, harsher penalties and increased use of police and troops to control student activities. In other words, student violence has everywhere been met with greater violence, rather than any serious attempt to discuss and deal with root causes. One sees police forces equipped with mace and tear gas; the fearsome weaponry and body armour of troops like San Francisco's Tactical Squad, small towns near 'tinder box areas' purchasing war surplus tanks for the use of their police forces. And since the police have been made the enemy in a sporadic guerrilla warfare, one cannot, in fairness, blame them for trying to protect their own lives. One learns that of all the registered hand-gun owners in the United States, over one-third at the present time are women. Perhaps, as in South Africa, afternoon meetings of the revolver club will supplant the bridge clubs and bowling clubs.[23]

The backlash is most notable at certain levels of society. The upper class and wealthy, the 'Establishment', particularly threatened, are able to take financial measures to safeguard their interests. Another level of society where the backlash is particularly felt is in the lower middle class and labouring groups who feel that students have an easy life, are not worthy of sympathetic support, and that student demonstrations should be put down at all costs. I would remind you of the recent episode in New York City where a group of peacefully demonstrating students were set upon by a gang of construction workers, the so-called 'hard-hats', and were brutally beaten. I had the experience of seeing two of these 'hard hats' interviewed on a late television show, and have never before encountered such frank hatred as these two men expressed for the students. By and large, the 'hard hats' tend to be war veterans of the Korean and Vietnam conflicts, trained to hate and trained to kill, distrustful of the intellectual, and with no sympathy whatsoever for the anti-war views of students.

One must record that there is in this country, and has been, since approximately the time of Lincoln, a latent fear of the intellectual; the term 'egghead' expresses the attitude. This latent fear would seem to be on the increase as students become more vociferous. Anyone listening to the speeches of the current Vice President of the United States will note how this fear is being played upon for political ends. The fear on the part of many university administrators is that the development of ultra-conservatism as an answer to the student revolt will result in the down grading, if not destruction, of the universities, and eventually lead to the institution of an American form of fascism. And finally one must admit that the idealist student activists would, if they succeeded in getting their own way, substitute a form of totalitarianism which is quite fascist itself in its disregard for the views of other people.[24]

The survey of violence in the American university scene, and in life generally, is not conducive to optimism. Most Americans realize that the road ahead is difficult and dangerous, and that their great country, which has meant so much to so many, is in for testing times. One bright spot, however, on the student scene must be documented, if only to show that a sense of humour exists and may yet save the day. On the campus of the University of Chicago, a group of students have banded together to form an organization called 'Students for Violent Non-Action'. These young people have, in the course of seeking to influence the university, carried out such things as nude 'swim-ins', for a splinter group which calls itself 'Students Krazy for Institutional Non-Denominational Diving Into Pools' (S K I N N I E D I P). They have handed out pollution kits for persons who are not so fortunate as to have pollution problems; this programme they call 'Grateful Americans Supporting Pollution' (G A S P). They have recently formed a Men's Liberation movement, which group is called 'Student Project for Equal Rights for Men' (S P E R M). They have formed, to 'assist' the Women's Liberation movement, a sisterhood known as 'Outraged Virgins Uniting for Men (O V U M). And finally, whenever the Students for a Democratic Society meet on the campus of the University of Chicago, the members of the S V N A dig trenches around the S D S meeting centre to 'protect the S D S from attacks by the National Guard'. Needless to say, the S V N A are not entirely popular with the S D S; they are unhappy that they have not been attacked; their president has recently said, 'We need repression to grow in power'. One good way to de-toxify a tense social situation is the good old-fashioned British method of 'taking the mickey'.

So what does all of this mean? In the opinion of this observer, as has already been stated, the principal element behind the furore of student unrest in the U S is the headlong collision between an out-moded, work-orientated, materialistic 'WASP' culture, shored up by certain institutions but perhaps, in the long context of mankind's history, already as dead as the dinosaur – and a new emerging culture which rejects many aspects of the old, substitutes a real concern for the feelings and rights and dignity of every human being, and is intolerant of all that stands in its way. Unfortunately, youth is always intolerant; today's youth, brought up in an 'instant' society, has not learned the meaning of patience. Does all of this mean that the U S is in for a blood bath? God forbid – surely we have learned by now that violent solutions seldom solve violent problems. Can pressure be brought peacefully to bear upon vested interests maintaining the status quo, to bring about change? One has only to look at the state of health of the tobacco industry (in the light of what we know about the causation of lung cancer) to achieve a certain degree of disillusion. Whether change will come by revolution or evolution remains to be seen; but come it will. Mankind's history suggests that there will not likely be a going back; the new wave cannot be suppressed forever. Perhaps the best that can be hoped for is that a sense of humour may somehow mitigate the possible disasters ahead. The United States, unlike Great Britain, does not have a reputation for the ability to work out compromise situations, but occasional vignettes of tolerance and humour – even the antics of the S V N A at the University of Chicago – make one dare to hope that perhaps, like Britain, the U S may also find a way of 'muddling through'.

References

1 Brown, Michael, Ed., *The Politics and Anti-Politics of the Young*. Glencoe Press, New York, 1969.

2 Flacks, Richard, *Transaction*, pp. 46-55, Vol. 7, No. 8, June, 1970.

3 Farnsworth, D. L., *Psychiatry, Education and the Young Adult*. Thomas, Springfield, Ill., 1966.

4 Farnsworth, D. L., *Psychiatric Opinion*, pp. 3-6, Vol. 6, No. 9, December, 1969.

5 Flacks, Richard, *Psychology Today*, Vol. 1 (6) pp. 18-23, October, 1967.

6 Halleck, Seymour L., *American Journal of Psychiatry*, Vol. 124 (5), pp. 642-650, November, 1967.

7 Daniels, D. N., Gilula, M. F., and Ochberg, F. M., Eds., *Violence and the Struggle for Existence*. Little, Brown, Boston, 1970.

8 Storr, A., *Human Aggression*. Atheneum, New York, 1968.

9 Berkowitz, L., *Aggression – a Social-Psychological Analysis*. McGraw-Hill, New York, 1962.

10 Bandura, A., and Walters, R. H., *Social Learning and Per-*

sonality Development. Holt, Rinehart and Winston, New York, 1963.

11 Keniston, K. in *Psychopathology of Adolescence.* (J. Zubin and A. Freedman, Eds.), Grune and Stratton, New York, 1970.

12 Miller, P. R., *Medical Opinion and Review,* Vol. 6, No. 11, pp. 63-65, November, 1970.

13 Harris, R., *New Yorker, Annals of Legislation.* Vol. 44, pp. 56, 58, 105, 20 April 1968.

14 Schmandt, H. J., and Bloomberg, Warner (Jr.) Eds., *The Quality of Urban Life.* Vol. 3, Urban Affairs Annual Reviews, Sage Publications Inc., Beverly Hills, California, 1969.

15 Barnett, S. A., *The Rat—a Study in Behaviour.* Aldine, Chicago, 1963.

16 Milgran, S., *Science,* Vol. 167, No. 3924, pp. 1461-1468, 13 March 1970.

17 Friedenberg, E. Z., *J. Social Issues,* Vol. 24 (2), pp. 21-38, 1969.

18 Gilula, M. F., and Daniels, D. N., *Reflections* (Merck and Company), Vol. V, No. 4, pp. 36-63, 1969.

19 Schram, W., Lyle, J., and Parker, E. B., *Television in the Lives of Our Children,* Stanford University Press, Stanford, California, 1961.

20 Wolfle, D., Editorial, *Science,* Vol. 167, No. 3924, p. 1441, 1970.

21 Himmelweit, H. T., Oppenheim, A. N., and Vince, P., *Television and the Child.* Oxford University Press, New York, 1958.

22 Distler, L. S., *Psychiatry,* Vol. 33, pp. 362-371, August 1970.

23 *American Rifleman, 116,* (Nos. 2-5) Various writings, 1968.

24 Eisenberg, L., *Science,* Vol. 167, No. 3926, pp. 1688-1692, 1970.

25 Chow, T. J., *San Francisco Examiner and Chronicle,* p. 20, September 13, 1970.

The contribution of the schools
Geraldine Lack

As Aldous Huxley said in *Ends and Means*: 'War is not a law of nature, nor even a law of human nature. It exists because men wish it to exist; and we know as a matter of historical fact that the intensity of that wish has varied from absolute zero to a frenzied maximum. The wish for war in the contemporary world is widespread and of high intensity, but our wills are to some extent free; we can wish otherwise than we actually do. It is enormously difficult for us to change our wishes in this matter, but the enormously difficult is not the impossible.'[1]

What is happening in the world is, as we can see, largely the result of attitudes of mind and convictions built into our culture and often accepted by us without thinking. But attitudes and beliefs can be changed. Their appeal is often emotional rather than intellectual and because of this they are difficult to modify in an adult population as a whole, but they can be discussed and reconsidered by the young. If we can find enough enlightened parents and teachers who believe that this is a first priority, if in spite of the welter of subject committees and curriculum studies we can convince at least some of the universities and administrators and teachers that the curriculum must be considered not piecemeal but as a whole, and with building up sound human values as the paramount consideration, then we can really begin again with the rising generation. To repeat

Huxley: 'The enormously difficult is not the impossible', and if ever a time called for an effort on the part of every thinking person it is now.

What makes our task particularly urgent is that this generation of young people faces a world unlike any that young people have ever faced before. It is perhaps the most exciting world that any generation has met, but unfortunately it is also the most dangerous. This may seem a big claim to make, but the difference lies of course in the pace of change. The difference also lies in the pace at which man is acquiring his knowledge of the universe, and in the enormous powers which are becoming available to him as a result of this knowledge: weapon power, power to change his environment, power over men's minds, power to create a new kind of human being, power to destroy the world as we know it. The pace of change means that there is not time to acquire the understanding which will enable him to make use of these powers for good rather than for evil.

As a result of this situation not only young people but older ones too have a feeling of helplessness. What can any individual do? What can 'we' do? Is there anything left but to hope that we can live out our own little lives in comparative peace and happiness? For the young this is not so easy. Some opt out, some rebel, some try to get together, but for what? There is also the feeling of despair at the facelessness of the 'they' who make use of these great powers, who take these great decisions as to how the resources of the country in money or manpower are to be spent. In space research? In defence? Or in feeding the starving millions of the world? 'They' make wars. 'They' make the ultimate decisions. 'They' prevent any changes in our educational policy. Who are 'they' – men or computers or a mixture of both? What can 'we' do?

What we can do is to get together and begin in our schools, colleges and universities to establish the kind of society that we want. Societies which have consciously attempted something of this kind – for instance, Hitler's Germany with a pattern of values deliberately nationalistic and militaristic, Russia with her deliberate indoctrination of youth with the ideals of Communism, China at the present time with a set of values opposed to the materialistic, and city-centred societies of the West – all have attained a considerable measure of success by concentrating on educating their young people. They have shown what can be achieved when the efforts and resources of a society are primarily directed towards building up for the young a set of values which they come naturally to accept.

While obviously none of us would be prepared to follow the example of these totalitarian societies in indoctrinating the young, yet we can learn from them. If we want to change the values of our society, we must begin talking about this with our young people even at school age, discussing controversial issues with them, and working with them to try to find solutions to our problems, both national and international.

The battle in some ways is already half won. There is no need to persuade the young to challenge the convictions of their elders – disbelief in their values is already general; but we have not provided them with a constructive alternative and we have not trained them to think intelligently about current political and social problems. All they know is that they do not like their society as they see it; they want to contract out, to 'make love not war', to 'do their own thing'. Somehow parents and educationalists and teachers must try to provide a pattern of education based on ideals in which they and the young can both believe.

It may be said that if we do this deliberately we are embarking, whether we want to or not, on a course of indoctrination – a course which is dangerous and which we deplore when we see it in operation in countries whose values we dislike. The answer must be that some kind of indoctrination of the young is going on all the time far more strongly and insistently than we should ever pursue it. We all know the dangers of the 'hidden persuaders', but now on all sides are the open persuaders as well, in books and theatres, high-pressure advertising and the mass media. The battle with these forces, or rather with those who are corrupting the media, must be joined using all the resources at our command.

Many people will also question the possibility of the schools achieving such a radical change of attitude, given the complexity of our modern society. How far can we bring about change in society when we no longer have values and beliefs in common? In authoritarian societies this is more possible because life forms a coherent whole and because authority is not questioned: are there for us any principles upon which we are all agreed and by which man can live? Because if there are, it is upon these that we must build our schools.

Here the one answer that can be given is the one which surely every human being must accept if our race is to survive – 'loving our neighbours'. Whether the interpretation of this Christian ethic takes a Christian form or a humanist one is not of importance, for the humanist demand for respect for every individual as an individual, regardless of race, creed or colour – and this includes self-respect – is saying the same thing. It is this basic principle which lies behind the virtues to which we all at least pay lip-service – justice, compassion, awareness of those who need help, and sensitivity. With it of course must also go honesty of mind, and perhaps courage, because if we are going to live by this principle we must genuinely believe in it and we must have the courage to give expression to our belief in words as well as behaviour. It must become the groundwork of everything that is done in education.

Nevertheless this raises another question: how is this kind of discussion possible in the present climate of opinion? Neither teachers nor parents are sufficiently clear in their own minds about what they think is important, nor are they very happy about discussing their own basic values or making these explicit to each other and to the children without cynicism or embarrassment. A great many adults now are too mentally sophisticated for discussion of this kind. They are uncomfortable about speaking out in public and afraid of sounding too pious or too obvious or too simple. They are afraid of saying in front of friends and colleagues, or even to children, what needs to be said about goodness, about concern for others, or about the evils of war. Children need a directness and simplicity of approach in discussions of this kind that many teachers, and also parents, have lost, but must recover if they are to communicate with them. Words after all are one of the chief means of human communication and must be used, dangerous though they are. One of the most delightful and really good headmistresses that I knew – 'good' in the sense that we have just been using the word, in that she really practised 'loving her neighbour' – failed as a headmistress because she never explained to the children what she believed in. We all know that words are not enough and that deeds must support them. In these days there is equally a danger in forgetting that deeds are not enough; words must support them. So the first principle that we can lay down for education in schools is that we must be prepared to put into words again and again what we believe in, to each other, to parents, and to children, and then must relate everything we do, including behaviour towards each other, to what we believe. Once when a sixth-former was asked about her school her answer showed that something of this had been achieved; she said 'But ours isn't a school, it's a way of life', and it is a 'way of life' that we need to establish.

What then are the specific contributions that first parents and then the schools themselves can make towards building up values and beliefs of the kind we need?

Perhaps before thinking about this, it is as well to make clear that schools are well aware that they can do very little where the parents are either antagonistic or indifferent to their aims. Unfortunately in some areas this is the state of affairs and here, whatever the school tries to do, in the end the influence of the home or the neighbourhood usually prevails. The prejudices of the home are repeated in the child. But if we are to reform our society we must begin somewhere, and the most hopeful place will be with the schools where home and school and children are working together. It is only to those who realize this that this chapter will make sense. The parents then can help by thinking very much more carefully about the function of education. They have taken the old patterns for granted far too long, and have too often brought pressures to bear on the schools to achieve the kind of academic successes which are part of the competitive materialistic society from which we need to escape. They should help the schools, as long as they continue to exist in their present form, to see that their function is not just to teach subjects, but, with the parents, to engage in fruitful dialogue with the young about the kind of urgent problems that the world is now facing, and to help them to understand what being a member of the human race really means. This demands much more emphasis on school as a community and much less on school as a place for study or a cramshop for passing examinations. After his home, school is the first community to which a child belongs. His beliefs about what is right and what is wrong, what is worth struggling for and what is not worth bothering about, are largely established before he leaves it.

Parents in choosing a school, or in meeting the Head and the staff, should surely be asking questions about opportunities for discussing with the school the values it is trying to instil. They have a right to know for instance what the school is doing towards sending children out with a belief that asking for what you want with anger and violence can only beget more anger and violence, and that war can only end in the final destruction of the human race. They can ask what new thinking has gone into the curriculum, and what pattern of relationships exists within the school. They will also do everything in their power to co-operate with the school. Not all parents understand what this really means. Their sense of responsibility will involve a certain number of them in sociable fund-raising activities, but they find it hard to accept the ideas that education should be a genuine partnership between school and parents, that parents and school form two halves of the same educational process, and that if the two halves fall apart the child suffers. Genuine co-operation means spending time with the school in discussing objectives and ends, and in creating the kind of community in which they both believe.

If this then is to be the parents' contribution, what are we asking of the schools? There are two main tasks. The first is the building up of a relevant curriculum, in a genuine attempt to give the adolescents some knowledge of the problems of the world into which they are going; this is particularly necessary in view of the fact that with children of school age opportunities for international contacts and foreign travel are necessarily limited. The second task is to make the values in which we believe part of their actual experience in the day-to-day life of the school.

First, then, the curriculum: the schools must, as indeed many of them are doing, put the demands of the examination system into their true perspective. If they had not been so rigidly controlled by these in the past they could have experimented more, evolved differently, become more free and more equal communities. More than this: without our altogether realizing it, the examination system has imposed on the public, the parents, the teachers and the children themselves, the idea that intellectual values are the most important ones and that only children who can pass examinations are destined to succeed. Those who cannot, fail. And yet we know that intellectual excellence is only one of many values. People can be endowed with many different gifts of personality and character, of creativity in art and music and literature, or of forming satisfactory human relationships – and yet at school the all-important success must come through passing examinations, and examinations moreover designed to select candidates for university entry. How is it that a society which later comes to distrust intellectual values (look at the American's attitude to the 'egghead') and is suspicious of the influence of intellectual values in government or in business, should lay such enormous stress on them at the school stage? This attitude is producing frustration and misery among those whose gifts do not lie in this direction, and often an emphasis on wrong values among those who do. We know that the people who have done most for the world have not necessarily been the most academic pupils at school, and yet we find this frantic pressure from parents and teachers to exclude from the curriculum anything which will interfere with the passing of examinations. Somehow we must convince parents and, more important still, the boys and girls themselves, that examinations are our servants not our masters, that they have their uses but are fallible, and that values other than academic must have their place and importance in the schools.

Instead then of being completely tied, as so many of them are, to the present examination-dominated curriculum, the teachers, with the other educational bodies concerned, must obviously devise, and probably at national rather than local level, a curriculum that will help young people, firstly, to understand some of the economic and social problems of their own country – this racially mixed and class-divided society, in which the unskilled and inadequately educated are likely to be without work; and secondly, to think internationally. The adolescents are at the age when ideals are of tremendous importance to them: they *want* to be given an understanding of the different kinds of contribution that each individual can make to the common good, and to the growth of a world society which alone can assure them of a future, and give meaning and direction to their lives.

95

Examples of the kind of topic that they wish to discuss and should be discussing are the causes of war mentioned at the beginning of the chapter. How far, for instance, has the teaching of national history to school children conditioned them to fight for their countries, right or wrong? School histories have been preoccupied with the gains or losses and the internal policies of nation states. Far too little attention has been given to cultural diffusion, especially with regard to science and technology. There is little doubt that the teaching of history could be so altered that the children could be taught to believe in the interdependence of all mankind, and to differentiate between patriotism and the bellicose nationalism that has so often in the past contributed to war.

Another of the important issues of our time which must certainly be found a place in the discussion lessons is the exploitation of natural resources in the world, especially those in short supply. This may be the only occasion in their lives when the young will be encouraged to look dispassionately at the facts and consider their implications, and yet this kind of exploitation is one of the most likely causes of war and is certainly an example of behaviour in direct opposition to the values in which we profess to believe.

Religious teaching, which is still compulsory in our schools, should also perhaps be treated in a different way. The young should be brought to understand what a divisive force religion and creeds have been and can be (the present situation in Ulster is a case in point) and that although religion is, rightly, of great significance in many people's lives, nevertheless intolerance and bigotry, so often dangerously associated with it, can be one of the major causes of war. It is of the utmost importance that adolescents should realize this danger.

In the time devoted to scientific work and study much more emphasis will have to be given to the population explosion and the part it is playing in provoking war. The urgency of the need for family planning and birth control must be brought to the attention of the adolescent and must not be left until he is adult, particularly in view of the earlier maturing of the young. Equally the young will have to understand the necessity of providing access to the under-populated areas of the earth, and the national conflicts this will provoke unless there is a general understanding of the problems involved.

Theirs too is a world in which the scientific revolution is threatening their very existence. They need to be led to understand, for instance, the implications for man of the new weapons, and of 'the biological time bomb', and the pollution of our environment. They need more understanding of psychology and of the growth of human societies. Discussion of topics such as these and constructive suggestions for international co-operation in solving the problems must clearly play a big part in their curriculum.

If the curriculum is going to be centred round discussions and activities such as these there will have to be great changes in the pattern of secondary education. We have perhaps for too long been spending our energies on the reorganization of schools without being sufficiently concerned about what is happening in them.

There is, as I said, an obvious need for making examination teaching less important and perhaps relegating it to the last two or three years of school life, and even at that stage giving it only a portion of the time available. This will leave the first four or five years of the secondary school course free for experiments in the curriculum. Such experimental studies fall naturally into four groups. Firstly, there are the humanities and social sciences, based on the study of man and society. The Schools Council definition in Working Paper No. 2 makes their purpose clear – 'to forward understanding, discrimination and judgment in the human field' which will involve 'reliable factual knowledge, ... direct experience, imaginative experience, some appreciation of the dilemmas of the human condition and the rough-hewn nature of many of our institutions, and some rational thought about them'.[2] Secondly, there will be a group of scientific studies, and much of the work done in this field will belong, as the Working Paper puts it, 'to the same family of thinking'. These studies too will include 'man, his environment and the questions of human behaviour and value which scientific method can help and illuminate'. This work will be linked to the first group also by its specific emphasis on the implications for man of new developments in science and technology. Thirdly, there must also be a place for creative activities, for music and art and the special interests of the individual. This is not only because these activities are an essential part of human experience, but also because if we are to avoid war we must help to produce a society of well-balanced creative people who have learned to rely on themselves for their entertainment and leisure-time pursuits, and are not completely dependent on the mass media, with their attendant dangers, for filling empty lives. Lastly of course there must be a place for special skills such as mathematics and language.

Teachers are already finding that where a curriculum of this kind is planned there is a need for a greater interrelation of subjects, and for team work among the staff rather than for the old pattern of subject teachers concerned only with the subject disciplines. They are breaking away from traditional time tables, with their forty-minute periods, and using blocks of time allocated to different kinds of activities and studies. Project work of all kinds is being developed, much of it exciting and valuable, as the working papers of the Schools Council, the Nuffield and Stenhouse projects, the General Studies project at York University and many other similar experiments are showing. The Schools' Broadcasting services are aware of the problems and are contributing most valuable programmes. What is needed now is to make the knowledge of these experiments more widespread, and to make this kind of approach a primary concern in the training of all teachers.

For too long we have allowed all these different experiments to develop in the rather haphazard fashion that is perhaps characteristic of England with its insistence on the freedom of the teacher to develop his own curriculum. Even the Nuffield research groups, for instance, developed their programmes in each science separately with very little concern for what the others were demanding of the schools. Surely in the present situation there should be an attempt to suggest what values, what ideas, what problems need urgent reconsideration by the whole of our society.

These must not be left for the consideration of the adult population only, but must be made part of the education of every growing child. This does not imply a dictated curriculum worked out in detail for all our schools. Each country and each part of the country has its own problems, and those will clearly affect what we do with the children. Children themselves have different needs and teachers have differing aptitudes, and these again must be taken into account by the schools. Nevertheless a real attempt to create a basic curriculum, relevant to the needs of our time, should be made in all schools. We need to bring the varied and individual curriculum experiments together to see what we can learn from them, and we must make a genuine effort to provide the teachers with the training, books, materials and teaching aids for their very difficult task.

What will be demanded of them as people will also change. What is needed in the teachers is not so much academic ability, though this is useful, as other qualities even more important. A curriculum of this kind first demands hard work, constant reading and thinking, and absolute honesty in their approach to the problems they are discussing, and the willingness to think the problems through to the best of their ability – not always an easy task; secondly, the courage to be prepared, if asked, to make some sort of commitment. They cannot help young people if they remain sitting on the fence. Lastly, if a commitment is made, then the third quality demanded of them is humility, because the young have a right to reject their point of view, provided that the rejection is made with courtesy and with reasons to support it.

There are two difficulties that we may have to face if we hope to implement a programme of this kind: one is the attitude of the universities, and the other is the revolution in teaching methods which began in the primary schools and is now beginning to make an impact at the secondary stage.

The universities will no longer be able to rely only on examinations of the traditional kind for the selection of their students; but does this matter? New methods of evaluation and appraisal are now being worked out in connection with CSE, and have been in use in other countries for some time. They will prove more satisfactory, perhaps, than the methods of Advanced and Ordinary Level papers with their greater reliance on memory and recapitulation of facts learned by rote. Then, too, the universities may have to cover more of the preparatory work in particular subjects now done in schools; but surely this can be done more quickly and effectively by them with more adult students if only because of the difficulty the teachers now have in keeping up with the changing content of subjects? Also, because the demands of the young will be for the more relevant, man-centred curriculum already suggested, the universities may find that certain of the Departments – for example, Classics, Archaeology, possibly some of their History courses, and some Literature and Linguistic courses – may have to become postgraduate studies, rather than occupy the position of importance that many of them now have in the First Degree Course.

The second difficulty is that in many of the schools where there has been a great desire to break away from traditional patterns of education, too much emphasis is being laid on method and not enough on content. This is a natural development from the revolution that has taken place in our primary schools, where the emphasis in education is now rightly on enquiry, on the problem-solving approach, on doing, and on the active participation of the child. The aim of the teacher has been to make the school a good place to live in, where what is taught is only of secondary importance. All this has been of great value at the primary school stage and cannot but be a force for good at the secondary stage too, but is it enough? Its influence has been of value in drawing attention to the personal development of the child, to relationships and to what the learning process should be, and it has rightly begun to undermine our traditional ideas about authority, the value of subject disciplines and the need for an all-embracing examination system. This again can do nothing but good, but again is it enough?

Too much emphasis on method, too much time given to activity and enquiry, enjoyable though they may be for the child, can be a waste of time. They must have their place and importance in the school day, but, particularly in the secondary school, there is also still a place for class teaching and discussion and dialogue with the teacher. If there is mutual confidence between the generations, and this is what we must and can establish, it should be natural for the child to take some ideas and facts for granted, even if these are only a jumping-off ground for critical enquiry later. He cannot find out everything for himself, and with our present world situation there is not time. No generation can regard its beliefs as infallible but each rising generation must, if it is to advance at all, build on the foundations given to it without pulling all the bricks apart and starting again. Old and young must work together, using what each has to give.

More than this, our students, working with us, must understand what we are trying to do. They must be partners. Too many now leave school without any understanding of what their education has been about; their school work appears to them to be completely irrelevant to their lives. At every stage of their school experience there is a need to make the purpose of what we are doing clear to them.

I have spent some time on the curriculum because there is a great deal to be done here, but perhaps even more important is the second task of the schools that was mentioned: 'to make the values in which we believe a part of the experience of young people in the day-to-day life of the schools'. It is difficult to explain what is meant by this without giving some specific details, so I should like to describe very briefly what happened in one school where an attempt of this kind was made. This was a girls' day school in England, and the whole process started about eighteen years ago – long enough for the school to see some results. It began with some limited experiments in the Sixth Form curriculum, of the kind I have mentioned. I shall not describe these, except to say that in spite of cutting down on examination teaching to about half time, the University entry improved steadily, and that there was an overwhelming wish on the part of the girls for the General Studies Course which was provided as the centre of the Sixth Form curriculum. What was more important however was the attempt made by the staff to make the basic values on which all societies must be founded, if human beings are to survive, a reality in the life and organization of the school, and to give the girls the genuine freedom and responsibilities appropriate to their age. They also worked in close co-operation with the parents.

The giving of freedom and the taking of responsibility had to begin with the First Years, not with the Sixth. The staff realized that you cannot expect people of sixteen to use their freedom well without previous experience and training, any more than the Universities are finding that they can expect their students to be mature and to accept responsibility unless the schools have already given them experience in taking it. Learning to live in a free community and to take responsibility must be a continuous process and a very important part of growing up. As we have seen so clearly in this century, in any country where the discipline of the schools is too rigid and authoritarian, even though the general aims of the school may be good in other ways, the conditioning of the child is likely to produce the conformist adult. He becomes the natural victim of the leader who has the ability to set in motion the conditioned response of unthinking loyalty to authority, even where the actions of the authority are dangerous or evil and may lead to war. If we are to avoid this, we must give the children the opportunity of taking genuine responsibility and of making choices and decisions which they can see will affect their lives.

The staff found that the best method of achieving this was through the School Council – not a girls' council, but one consisting of a member from every form, and of Sixth Form and staff representatives. This began to play a very big part in the life of the school. The girls really had the chance of sharing in the school's organization and government. The resolutions coming from every age-group were discussed and voted on, and helped to determine the pattern of their lives. More than that, the girls were learning all the time by practical experience such lessons as why rules had to be made, how different sections of the community had to consider each other, what say minority groups ought to have when voted down in the full council. Form Committees and a Sixth Form Council gave still further opportunities for discussion and action, but in whatever they did staff and girls worked and planned together and consequently the pattern of relationships altered. The school became a community in which mutual respect, consideration, and intelligent and shared planning of the life of the community replaced the old authoritarian pattern.

All of this naturally meant a much more explicit consideration of the values on which the community life of the school was based. Again the process had to begin with the first-year entry. It was necessary to make clear even to the youngest girls that the really important lesson to be learned in school was how to live with other people and consider them. As they grew older their sympathies and understanding of the needs of others must grow too, but this had to be developed within the situation experienced by the girls. In the lower forms they were encouraged to think more of what they could do to help in their homes and to recognize both the contributions and the needs of each section of the school community – the girls, the prefects, the domestic staff and the teaching staff. By the time they reached the middle school they were encouraged to become more aware of the difficulties of their own peer groups, and of the needs of the local community. Finally, when they reached the Sixth Form their discussions, their reading, the films that they saw, the conferences they attended, and their journeys abroad gave them some understanding of international problems and relationships which we all of us need to develop if we are to create one world.

What the staff had failed to do in the past had been to communicate these values to the children. Now, by explicit discussions, and by making these values implicit in the organization and relationships within the school, they could give to its daily life a unity and meaning and an excitement – for planning together is exciting – which had never existed before.

Just as the school had failed to communicate with the children, so it had failed to communicate with parents. The last of the tasks of the staff was to learn to work constructively with them too. They brought them to school before their daughters arrived and again in the first year to explain that they would like if possible to work with them at all stages of their daughters' lives at school. They told them that they would get into touch with them straight away if they were concerned about any aspect of their daughters' health or progress, and hoped that the parents would keep them equally informed of anything happening at home that was likely to affect them. They asked for their loyalty and support in so far as to suggest that if they had criticisms of the school and its values, these should be made to them, not to their daughters; otherwise a child was made to feel insecure and uncertain of which set of values was right. From the moment this conflict of values was apparent to the girl, from that moment the school ceased to be able to help her. With the middle school parents the staff began to discuss the pressures which they found were affecting their daughters – pressures from peer groups, advertising, and other mass media – and suggested that they should form groups with the parents of their daughters' friends, to decide between them what standards they would ask for. Equally before the girls started on the General

Studies course in the Sixth Form they brought the parents of the sixth formers together to explain what they were doing. Working with the parents and genuinely communicating with them was a necessary part of everything that was done in school.

This kind of experiment I have been describing in making sense out of school life, in a genuine communication with both child and parent, and in making school a place to live in, not only to be taught in, is now being tried in many other schools too, but far more needs to be done if we are going to create a society in which was is outlawed, and to provide anything approaching a relevant educational system for our children before the year 2000. We need a change of outlook among many of our administrators who accept the system as it stands, and who, while they do everything they can to see that the teachers are given help and encouragement within the system, still have not realized that the system itself is outdated and must be changed.

If we are to help young people in this very exciting, rapidly changing and extremely dangerous world of 1970 to 2000 we must once again, as so often in the history of man, do some radical rethinking about the whole purpose and content of education. But we must do it soon because in every way time is short.

References

1 Huxley, Aldous (1937), *Ends and Means*. Chatto and Windus. pp. 93-4.
2 The Schools' Council (1965), *Working Paper No. 2*. Raising the School Leaving Age. H M S O pp. 14 & 20.

The concept of maturity
David A MacSweeney

Psychological, intellectual, emotional and physical development do not proceed at the same pace in any given individual; any or all these areas of development may become either temporarily or permanently arrested. Some years ago a Peruvian girl of five and a half was successfully delivered of a baby by Caesarean section; while she was physically equipped for child-bearing, she was unlikely to have been emotionally or intellectually capable of coping with the rearing of her child. We frequently see analogous if less dramatic examples of uneven development in the people about us. A person with a brilliant intellect may be pathetically inadequate in coping with human relationships. A brilliant surgeon may be embarrassingly naïve socially. A schoolboy of fifteen may have an intelligence quotient equivalent to that of a boy of nineteen; he may have the 'emotional age' of a boy of fifteen, or an adult of twenty, or indeed a child of ten. A psychiatrist may be a first-rate clinical diagnostician and a competent psychotherapist but at the same time be incapable of maintaining an adult emotional relationship with his own wife.

Before proceeding further I should like to describe what I mean by a normal person. I regard as normal anyone with near average intelligence who copes fairly consistently with his family, his work and his social commitments and enjoys being alive. This description rules out any gross (life-curtailing) neuroticism.

Raul Vispo[1] lists the following qualities which have been ascribed to the mature person by twenty-one authors who have written on this subject:

Harmony with environment and/or with oneself
Independence
Acceptance of reality
A system of moral values
Acceptance of responsibility
Adjustment to genital level of psychosexual development
Adaptability
Parental and creative abilities
Capacity for object relationship based upon differentiation of
   the object
Insight or self-knowledge
Consistency in personality
Tolerance
Outreach
Periodic regressions
Management of aggression
Management of anxiety
Self expression
Ability to delay action
Inner freedom
Capacity for the primordial act of wonder

To this list I should like to append two more:

Outrage and
Global kinship

Most of these writers include the first six items on this list, few consider any one particular quality the essential one and only one item, the last, is listed by Boelen. It is surprising that only three refer to what I consider one of the more important qualities—management of aggression.

Before elaborating further on these qualities I should like to stress that in the mature person you look for much more than you find in the normal person I have described above. Human

106

maturity is essentially a concept of the total personality; thus the observation of one isolated performance does not tell much more about the person than observing the actor, while acting, tells us about what the actor is like back-stage. The more or less consistent life-style of the person must therefore be taken into account. Vispo stresses the importance of observing both the internal and external behaviour of the individual. I hope then that it will become clear that maturity must be described not only from a social or external behaviour point of view but also from an internal or intra-psychic viewpoint.

Harmony with the environment and with oneself means that the mature person is not only on good terms with himself but also with the people he works with, with the other members of his family and with his friends. This does not mean that he is submissive, but he does however possess a degree of general adaptability.

By independence is meant that he is able to arrive at his own conclusions and not just present an amalgam of the opinions he has heard expressed by others; in other words he is sufficiently self-confident to think things out for himself having listened critically and selectively to the opinions of others.

Acceptance of reality means to be able to see one's immediate and long term prospects in terms of one's abilities, faults and achievements, to be able to distinguish wishful thinking from the feasible, to be able to confront the ineluctable drabness of life as it is with its haphazard joys, its frequent frustrations and its very occasional jigs of happiness.

A system of moral values means that the person maintains ideals and permanent standards of behaviour in his dealings with others. He accepts responsibility for his actions, his decisions and for those under his care. He never runs away though he may often feel like it.

Adjustment to genital level of psychosexual development simply means that a mature person has a capacity not only for receiving love on a permanent basis from a person of the opposite sex but is also capable of returning that love in a generous wholehearted manner. He is capable of enjoying the physical side of sex for its own sake but also recognizes in it the symbolic total giving of two people in a simple physical manoeuvre of mutual trust.

A mature person is adaptable. He is not rigid and stereotyped in his behaviour. He is not a stuffed shirt. He is good company in any company. He is rarely condescending and then only consciously so and only to the intellectually pompous.

Parental and creative abilities mean that he is able to pass his knowledge on to the young in an interesting way. If he is a parent he permits his children to explore the world about them without fretfully curtailing their every adventure. He can on occasion find new ways of evoking his offspring's interest and of expanding the repertoire of those interests.

Capacity for objective relationship based upon differentiation of the object simply means that the mature person is able to take an interest in and to love others and not be permanently wrapped up in narcissistic self-love. He is able to forget himself appropriately in the interests of others.

Insight or self-knowledge is most important; it means that a person is aware of the chinks and kinks in his own psychic apparatus. He has a fair degree of understanding of his own personality type, and of his ambitions, which are realistic and related to his natural endowment and special training. His personality is consistent; he does not have major mood swings so that at one time he is elated by minor good fortune and at another time depressed by an equally minor 'catastrophe'.

Tolerance, Vispo points out, means two things – to be able to tolerate tensions, frustrations and failures without panic or intensive depression. Secondly, it means that we are tolerant of others and their ideas, even when they are different from ours, *but* – we do not permit ourselves, in spite of this tolerance, to be pushed around intellectually, morally or physically.

Outreach is an Americanism which means that life for the mature person is always increasing in range and in importance. He is constantly extending the horizons of his interests and he can reach beyond himself, so that he is sympathetic to and capable of putting himself in touch with the aspirations of others.

Periodic regressions simply means that he retains some childlike curiosity for play and fantasy and is not above doing his own bit of clowning on occasion – *dulce et decorum est descipere in loco* – it is good to have a jug of wine now and then.

A minimum of floating anxiety and aggression is permissible

even in the mature person. However he does possess the ability to relax at appropriate times and to permit his mind to wander over the various topics which interest him. With regard to aggression, this has to be sublimated in the right direction so that its energy is rechannelled into activities which are professionally and perhaps artistically acceptable. It also means that he is capable of using aggression when indicated without cover for defence purposes or alternatively withhold his aggression until the right moment. It is related to outrage which I shall comment on later.

Self-expression means to be able to communicate our feelings and our ideas to others. Ability to delay actions means that the mature person has long-term values in mind and does not invariably resort to short-term ones – Freud's reality principle versus the pleasure principle.

He has inner freedom. He is at peace with himself, he accepts himself as he is and is not trying at all times to project a false image of himself. He is confident enough in himself to admit his own failings without making a boring fetish of enlisting them to others. From this internal peace and inner freedom he develops an unsmug serenity, an acceptance of the good, the indifferent and the bad which he must confront daily. He is pleased he was born – he is a good animal.

Capacity for the primordial act of wonder simply means that the world about us constantly intrigues our interest, that we are capable even in old age of being astonished and delighted by the variety and ingenuity of the things we see and hear and feel, that life never becomes a chore and we never become blasé in the drab hope-castrating implication of that word.

The external qualities listed above are obviously related to the external world. The mature person accepts reality, is in harmony with the environment and though he is independent (because he is able to arrive at his own conclusions) he is nonetheless maturely dependent on others. He is capable of love at a truly genital heterosexual level. He is tolerant but does not suffer from a 'professional nice guy' complex. He is consistently responsible. He is able to express his ideas, feelings and emotions to others competently and he is not afraid or embarrassed to do so. He is creative; he uses his energy successfully for achievement and does not burn up his free energy in neurotic fumblings. He continues throughout life to be delighted by the things about him – even in old age he continues to wonder like a well-informed child. By outrage I mean that sensibility to injustice or humbug – at local bar or international level – which prompts you to strike a practical well-directed blow to redress the wrong rather than merely abreacting – 'unpacking your heart with words'. It is related closely to management of aggression. By global kinship I mean an unromantic feeling of biological and social empathy with people of every race (or racial mixture), colour or creed and the imagination at least to try to extend this kinship not only for example to white South Africans, bigoted or non-bigoted, but to ineffectual white and coloured people all over the world:

> 'See the unhealed grief
> in every mean and selfish act,
> finding sweetness even in the mealy mouth.'

It implicates a responsibility to give unobtrusive practical help, not charity, whenever possible, and the wit to realize you are only doing your brother a small favour and that you don't deserve any thanks.

Must we possess all the above external and internal qualities in order to be mature? Certainly not. Insight or self-knowledge or 'self-objectification' I regard as fundamental. Allport says:

'The man who has the most complete sense of proportion concerning his own qualities and cherished values is able to perceive their incongruities and absurdities in certain settings.'

He goes on to specify a very important aspect of this quality, 'a sense of humour' – the possibility to laugh at ourselves and the things we love – to see behind some solemn event the contrast between pretension and performance. (Psychiatrists are notoriously humourless and when they jest their jokes smell of the midnight oil.) Vispo writes:

'If we cannot or are afraid to face ourselves, our motives, our limitations and possibilities, how can we imagine that we are not going to distort external reality to our taste or needs? If we take ourselves too seriously we will lose sooner or later our sense of proportion, and then criticism will not be accepted in good faith and only adulations will satisfy.'

The person who has arrived at maturity is at peace with

110

himself – he accepts himself as he is – warts, beauty-spots and all. From internal peace will derive a contentment with life. Vispo has summarized internal qualities by saying that he will show a continuity or consistency in his personality, 'he is essentially genuine or congruent, he has a character structure'. This consistency in personality does not mean that the mature person will be perfect or that he will not suffer moments of regressive behaviour – sudden expressions of unjustified anger, a selfish reaction, momentary delusions of grandeur – however, the mature person will rectify his behaviour and recognize his mistakes without feeling that he is losing self-respect: the immature cannot. He must be able to be alone – to be able to be at peace with himself while alone and at the same time to be in full communion with life. When the immature are alone they are ill at ease; they are lonely. They have a continuous need to receive the unquestioning support and busy reassurance of others. Being able to be alone is to accept that our strength needs to come essentially from the quiet well of our own spiritual resources.

The social (external) and intrapsychic (internal) qualities discussed above may join to express in the mature individual what Allport calls a Unifying Philosophy of Life, that is, a system of goals and values that will give shape and reason to our existence. For some this may be altruism, for others a religious approach to life, or a true morality, or a sense of informed sincerity and a sense of truth. The word wisdom best summarizes this quality. Does religious belief exclude one from arriving at maturity? Far from it. The mature person not only confronts his own personal reality and the stark reality of his outside world but he does both with calm ulterior optimism. The Christian believer has Pope John, Dag Hammarskjöld, Teilhard de Chardin and T. S. Eliot quietly at his side – Darwin himself was a deeply religious man but lacked the *joie de vivre* of the true Christian. Religion or faith is to me, at any rate, a humble joyous optimistic act of imagination and thrust in the unknowable:

> 'O God you have exquisite taste,
> You never work in spasm or in haste
> To cower our aspirations or our hope.'

Personally I find myself in the embarrassing position of luke-warm agnostic, a chronic doubting Thomas; if Jesus were kind enough to visit me personally I would not only want to put my finger into his wounds but also want to check his pulse and blood pressure and take a full psychiatric history.

In summary, in a mature person I would expect to find at least the following: self-knowledge (insight), peace with one-self, independence, only a minimum of floating anxiety (i.e. anxiety for no obvious reason), integration in one's social group, a system of ethical values, acceptance of reality, a sense of humour, possibilities of self-expression and of wonder, outrage and global kinship.

I will try and end with a mournful cheer by quoting Bertrand Russell, the most brilliant child who ever lived to be nearly a hundred: [2]

'It does not do to live in memories, in regrets for the good old days, or in sadness for friends who are dead. One's thoughts must be directed to the future and to things about which there is something to be done. This is not easy; one's past is a gradu-ally increasing weight. It is easy to think to oneself that one's emotions used to be more vivid than they are and one's mind more keen. If this is true it should be forgotten, and if it is for-gotten it will probably not be true.'

Orson Welles says 'The little bee should always be making honey' (for others as well as for himself). We are probably the best animals that ever got up off their bellies and crawled out of the easy-going sea (dolphins should never have changed their minds again). We deserve to thrive for a little longer – good luck to us all – everywhere.

References

1 Vispo, R. H., *On Human Maturity*, Perspectives in Biology and Medicine, 1966.
2 Russell, B., *Portraits from Memory and other essays*. London: Allen & Unwin, 1956.

Women working for peace
Frances Elliott

What can an ordinary middle-class woman do to work for
peace? The evils underlying the drive to war are so many, so
overwhelming, so interwoven in institutions of society, that it
may seem impossible for any one person or any small group
to do anything significantly useful about peace. One cannot
help asking, 'Isn't it desirable to forget world problems so that
we can remain sane enough to get through our daily tasks?
Haven't we elected leaders to deal with world problems? Aren't
they more capable than we are?' Such thoughts must go through
everyone's mind and perhaps they occur to women more
frequently than to men. But there are also more encouraging
things to bear in mind. It has been said that if only one per cent
of all the people in the world wanted peace we would have it.
Even a small minority of humane, dedicated, inventive people
would have the potential to influence society for the better. The
Vietnamese women who visited Canada last year made the
heart-warming observation that peace work progresses by
simply winning over one person at a time.

It is my belief that for most of us working for peace (and all
that that means) can only be done within an organization: few
individuals have the courage, resources, and drive to accom-
plish anything significant alone. There are many women's peace
groups, such as the one to which I belong, *The Voice of Women*

– *La Voix des Femmes* (V O W) in Canada. In England and the United States there are *The Women's International League for Peace and Freedom* (W I L P F) and *Women Strike for Peace* (W S P). The following description of V O W may indicate the type of work, the satisfaction and the frustrations that one can expect from being a member of such a group.

V O W was founded in 1960 as a response to a mass meeting held in Toronto to protest against the atom bomb testing which was then causing the widespread dissemination of dangerous radioactive fall-out. W S P was born in the United States in the same year and for a similar reason. The membership of V O W consists of about 2 000 women from all the provinces of Canada : it has a constitution providing for national and provincial officers, annual meetings, etc. The aims of the organization are expressed in its constitution :

'To unite women in concern for the future of the world,
to help promote the mutual respect and co-operation among nations necessary for peaceful negotiations between world powers having different ideological assumptions,
to protest against war or the threat of war as a decisive method of exercising power,
to appeal to all national leaders to co-operate in developing methods of negotiation of matters affecting their national security and the peace of the world,
to appeal to all national leaders to co-operate in the alleviation of the causes of war by common action for the economic and social betterment of mankind,
to provide a means for women to exercise responsibility for the family of mankind.'

To implement these aims the following propositions were selected for special attention and agreed at national meetings of V O W :

'The Voice of Women – La Voix des Femmes should continue to press the Canadian Government to :

A 1 Withdraw from the North Atlantic Treaty Organization (N A T O).
2 Withdraw from North American Air Defence Command (N O R A D).

114

3 Not join the Organization of American States (O A S).

4 Stop the export of military material.

5 Contribute Canadian foreign aid through the United Nations and increase that contribution to one per cent of the Gross National Product.

6 Protest at the United States action in Vietnam and the continuation and extension of the war into Cambodia and Laos.

7 Protest at the Soviet invasion and occupation of Czechoslovakia and appeal to all national leaders to adhere to negotiation.

8 Stop research in chemical-biological warfare (C B W) in Canada and urge conversion of present research stations into antipollution centres.

9 State to the U S A and the world Canada's unalterable opposition to the deployment of an A B M system as a socially and militarily irresponsible action, wasteful of needed resources and conducive to heightened world tensions.

10 Establish diplomatic relations with the People's Republic of China and instruct the Canadian delegate to the United Nations to do everything in his power and to take all necessary steps so that the People's Republic of China will occupy its seat as a Charter member of the United Nations. (Canada and P R C have just agreed to establish diplomatic contact.)

11 As the only defence for Canadians is world peace, the V O W should urge the Canadian Government to create by act of Parliament a new special Disarmament Agency, reporting directly to the Minister of External Affairs to be responsible for Canadian disarmament and conversion to peaceful production. A broad public information programme should be part of the work of the Disarmament Agency.

12 That the Canadian Government should press strongly to terminate all underground nuclear testing and, at the Disarmament Conference, take initiative to bring a halt to all nuclear testing by U S S R, China, France, and the U S A.

The Voice of Women – La Voix des Femmes should contine to support:

B 1 The Canadian Broadcasting Corporation and its independence in programming against the interference of the government and pressure groups.

2 The Indian, Metis and Eskimo peoples in their striving for fair treatment.

3 A reduction of violence on television, and in other media, and in toys etc., and an increase in educational television with emphasis on creativity towards peaceful solutions.

4 All measures which will free Canada from economic, social, political and military control by the U S A. It is time to stop Canada's continuing acquiescence in U S imperialism by allowing U S bombers to be based in Canada and by the participation of Canada in chemical and biological warfare research.'

Methods of work

During the past ten years V O W has sent delegates to conferences of peace workers in many countries. They attended the Women's Conference in Paris in 1964 concerned with N A T O and opposition to Multi-lateral Force, visited Czechoslovakia in 1968 at the invitation of the Czechoslovak Women's Union, and Hanoi (one delegate) at the invitation of the Union of Vietnamese Women.

Many individual members of V O W, and especially the leaders, have made comprehensive studies of the problems that concern us and by now we have a sizeable library of briefs, pamphlets and documents on these subjects. These have been used as the bases for educational meetings for members and the public, and for discussion with representatives of the government. They have served also for other educational activities of many sorts, such as letter-writing campaigns to members of Parliament, for leaflets handed out at demonstrations on the streets or mailed to the public, for press releases and for radio and television programmes. On some occasions dramatic or attention-getting measures have been used to assure television or newspaper coverage for a demonstration. In general, our protests have been based on the appeal to reason and they have invariably been non-violent.

The National Office of V O W publishes a quarterly bulletin for the whole membership. This contains reports of work, educational articles, suggestions for activities and news of interest to the members. Each provincial group publishes a bulletin of more local concern.

All these activities depend on hours of labour, thinking,

116

worrying, studying, conferring, telephoning, writing, arranging for meetings, travelling and marching, making posters, raising money, typing, collating, mailing, licking stamps, etc. A person who joins our organization has the opportunity to participate in all these types of work, as also to initiate projects that appeal to her and certainly to learn a great deal about the country's pressing problems.

There is one member of V O W who works mostly on her own. Mrs. Claire Culhane, a middle-aged Canadian mother and grandmother who is by profession a nurse, served for six months in 1968 as an administrator in the Canadian Tuberculosis Hospital in Quang Ngai, South Vietnam. Her experience there of the ineffectiveness of the Canadian aid, and its subversion to the support of the Saigon régime, was greatly disturbing to her. She returned to Canada to report the corruption of the Canadian aid, the extent of Canadian involvement in the Vietnam war and Canada's close ties with the United States military forces. She is now working to publicize her information about the unjust nature of the Vietnam war and specifically to persuade the Canadian government to stop its support of the United States government in this war. Apart from speaking to many groups and initiating anti-war vigils and campaigns along with V O W, she has fasted alone on Parliament Hill in Ottawa and lived in a tent in Ottawa for nineteen days in freezing weather in order to meet members of Parliament and tell them her news. Recently she travelled across Canada and in parts of the United States, speaking to high-school students, church people, etc. Everywhere she has made opportunities to dramatize her message. Although it is difficult to measure her effectiveness, there is no doubt that she is a great inspiration and a powerful force for peace. Few could emulate her, but she has shown what one ordinary middle-class woman can do to work for peace.

Criticism of peace groups

In an article such as this designed to encourage women to work for peace, it may seem contradictory to discuss or even to mention the shortcomings or difficulties of peace group work, but I think it is realistic to do so. A person, who after some soul-searching has decided to give up time for organizational work, becomes very frustrated if she finds that she is not given a worthwhile task to do, or too many tasks, or that her associates are difficult to work with, or that the work is more concerned with maintaining the organization than with peace activities. There are always personal problems in working with any group, but there are special troubles in a group like ours which enlists middle-class women and which has such broad general aims (and not a more specific concern, like pollution). Such a group usually finds itself with a few dedicated workers but with a relatively large membership of rather half-hearted people. The efforts of the leaders get diverted into satisfying this membership, to providing them with well-run meetings, not too revolutionary activities, projects that make the membership feel satisfied that their organization has done something for peace but nothing that compromised their position in society. Education of the membership therefore becomes a major task. There are other frustrations to be expected from working in groups such as ours.

It is discouraging too to discover that there are dissensions between different peace groups, dissensions that arise from many causes – from ideologies such as Marxism, liberalism or Maoism – from differences of age – from nationality – from race – or from class in society. These differences often give rise to advocacy of quite opposite tactics – moderate or extreme, violent or non-violent. Such dissensions are so prevalent that the enemies of peace, and supporters of the military-industrial states, can easily plant their agents in peace groups to promote dissension. All these troubles can be used as excuses by uncommitted people to remain aloof from peace work.

Yet, while recognizing these discouraging aspects of peace work and the underlying corruption of many governments, no one should dare forget that survival is at stake. One must be optimistic. And it is possible to be so on the basis of something more than simple determination. Leaders of the peace movement are constantly searching for new visions and new methods of work. And analysts of the world situation can see certain hopeful trends and movements.

I should like to quote from an article in *The New Yorker* of 23 September 1970, which gives an amazingly profound analysis of the evils of the 'Corporate State':

118

'But for many of a new generation, those endowed with the most hope and vitality, the revelations (of the corruptions of the corporate state) have led not to more disaffection but to something that is more dangerous to the state – a new kind of consciousness. This consciousness understands the conditions more the way a painter or a writer would and is sensitive not merely to a set of political and public issues but also to the deeper ills that Kafka or the German expressionists or Dickens would have seen.... The new consciousness feels that if he is to be true to himself, he must repond with himself.... When enough people have decided to live differently, the political results will follow naturally and easily and the old political forms will be simply swept away in the flood.'

The above quotation suggests that taking on this *new way of living* may be the most significant contribution each person can make towards peace. In this context peace work should be re-defined as work towards justice. Taking on this new way of living would, I should think, mean accepting a personal challenge to be more socially responsible, to make some sacrifices for deprived people, to work with citizen's committees concerned with medical aid or housing aid for the poor, etc. It would mean, in broader terms, being more understanding of the needs of other people, in one's family, in the neighbourhood, in the country and acting upon this understanding in a helpful way. This new personal commitment might be an alternative to working in a peace group, especially if that means time-consuming work, but it should not rule out membership in a peace organization. In fact associating with like-minded people in meetings and reading their literature could serve as inspiration for this *new way of living.*

Prisoners of conscience
Eric Baker

The term 'Prisoner of Conscience' was invented by Amnesty International at the beginning of its career,[1] to describe the kind of men and women for whom it intended to work. Amnesty was launched in 1960 through an article which Peter Benenson wrote in *The Observer* under the heading 'The Forgotten Prisoner'. It is true that not all prisoners of conscience have been forgotten; in fact the names of some, like Sheikh Abdullah – the first to enjoy the gloomy distinction of being chosen as the symbolic Prisoner of the Year – have been very well publicized. Nevertheless, for every prisoner whose name is well known there are hundreds who have never been known outside their own small circle. In Amnesty's files they have begun as a name and a prison sentence; and only after painstaking enquiry by workers in England, Denmark, Australia or one of the other countries in which there are Amnesty groups, has the background of relatives, occupation, indictment and other details been filled in.

There is a famous chapter in Ecclesiasticus, 'But some there be which have no memorial ...' There follows a passage praising those who have lived worthily and died in obscurity. It is a phrase which might fittingly find a place on an Amnesty plaque erected somewhere in memory of those who have lived out many quiet years of their lives and ended them in equal obscurity if in greater agony. Although the names of several thousand prisoners of conscience are listed in Amnesty's files, this is only a fraction of the total number. There are hundreds (or thousands?) who are kept in prison in South Africa, where even to mention that a relative is imprisoned is illegal; the hundreds imprisoned in Greece where the régime of the Colonels has by torture, practised or threatened, managed to terrorize into silence all but the most courageous or most foolhardy; the thousands of prisoners in 'Categories A, B and C' in Indonesia, not even the names of whom are known, much less whether they would fall to be classified as prisoners of conscience; while as for China, Taiwan and some of the South American Republics – who knows? The list of countries could be prolonged until it included most (but fortunately, not all) of those inside and outside the United Nations.

When so many of the sovereign nations of the world hold in their prisons so many prisoners of conscience, the success achieved by Amnesty in either winning their release, or at least some amelioration of their condition, is the more remarkable. It can probably be attributed to three factors : firstly the major effort made to define the term 'prisoner of conscience' and thus to identify those for whom to work; secondly the extraordinary unanimity and pertinacity with which ordinary men and women have worked for those equally unknown, and thirdly an embryonic but quite undeniable force in international life which can only be called 'international public conscience'. Each of these deserves to be looked at in some detail; for the rapid expansion of the work on behalf of prisoners of conscience as a genuinely international concern, is one of the most remarkable features of the post-war world.

It is worth spending time to follow in some detail the evolution of the term 'prisoner of conscience', since it is out of the discussions around this key concept that the philosophy behind the work has been clarified. There are few successful voluntary movements which start with a definition of aims, which is clear and never needs to be reworked. For most, the beginning is a powerful but somewhat incoherent hunch that here is a job to be done. What precisely the job is, and what the most effective way of doing it, is something which emerges only slowly as problem after problem is solved. The work for prisoners of conscience has been no exception. Time and again discussion inside Amnesty International has been concerned as much with the implications of the central concept as with questions of method. In practice, there has been little difficulty in providing a provisional definition and in pointing to the kind of people whose imprisonment was felt to be an injustice – the elderly Turk who wrote an article expressing mild socialist opinions, a Spanish priest who supported Basque nationalism, a schoolboy who made unfavourable comments about his own government in East Germany – acts and comments which in Britain or the United States would pass unnoticed. The difficulty has been to define more clearly the limits of the concept, to decide what was marginally in and what marginally out. This, in turn, led to a more fundamental question, that of the criteria by which 'acceptable' and 'unacceptable' behaviour on behalf both of the citizen and of the government should be decided.

Perhaps it would be best to take the latter first. Since the movement started in Britain, it was only natural that the standard which the founders had in mind was that observed in the conduct of public affairs in this country. It was not surprising, perhaps, that this was easily accepted in Western Europe, USA and in Australia and New Zealand. It was not surprising either that it was looked at askance in many other parts of the world to which Amnesty sought to apply it. Too often the attitude was that of a Minister of the Press who remarked shaking his head regretfully, 'Censorship is unfortunately necessary here. Our country has not the long tradition of stability that yours has, and we cannot afford the luxury of a free press.'

It was, therefore, necessary to find some criterion which could be appealed to and which at the same time could not be so easily dismissed by a government which found it inconvenient. Fortunately, one was to hand in the United Nations Declaration of Human Rights which, in sections 18 and 19 gave international recognition to just those freedoms of speech, assembly and worship which prisoners of conscience were being denied and which, therefore, it was necessary to seek to guarantee.[2] The Declaration itself is, it is true, no more, but also no less, than a statement of ideals. The Covenants which should give it legal (and, if ratified, binding) effect, are still, most of them, in the making. Nevertheless, what is of crucial importance is that the Declaration is not identified with one particular national culture but is the outcome of agreement by an international body. To work within its framework, therefore, is both to avoid the charge of cultural imperialism and to preempt the plea of cultural underdevelopment.

Having decided the criteria by which Amnesty's work should be guided, the next step was to apply them to particular situations. Here arises a major problem; almost no country will admit to holding prisoners of conscience in their gaols. A Roman Catholic priest may be held in a Communist country, not for trying to promote his faith but, ostensibly for transgression of currency rules; while the official interpretation of the term 'Communism' under which prisoners are held in South Africa is as wide as the Indian Ocean itself.

It is necessary, therefore, to scrutinize carefully the terms of a prisoner's indictment and to test whether the law under which he is held is one within or at odds with the spirit of the Declaration of Human Rights. Indeed, the scrutiny has been extended further, since it has become clear that not only the morality of the law itself but the validity of the evidence produced to convict a man of having transgressed that law, may itself be suspect. The suspicion is by now sufficiently well documented to have become a reasonable certainty that in a number of countries 'confessions' have been obtained by torture and, when the charge of brutality having been made, the court makes no attempt to test it, then there is unquestionably a very strong doubt whether the prisoner has been justly sentenced after a fair trial.

Sometimes, of course, a man is not 'imprisoned', in the strictest sense of that term. The means of rendering him impotent are numerous in any moderately well organized bureaucracy. One of the best known is the South African procedure of putting a man or woman under house arrest in circumstances which so strictly prevent his meeting others that he may even find it difficult to join in his own children's birthday parties. There is also the Russian procedure of not sentencing a man to prison, but of confining him to a mental hospital. The same purposes can be served by exile to a remote village or by depriving a man of the papers he needs to obtain employment.

In work for prisoners of conscience, it has been felt necessary to interpret the term as covering primarily those who are confined within an institution (although not always, since those under house arrest in South Africa have frequently been included). This decision has been taken as a matter not of principle but of expediency, there being far more prisoners even within the narrow interpretation than can easily be 'adopted'. The most painful decision has been to know what to do when a man is released from formal imprisonment, perhaps as a result of Amnesty's efforts. While he was in prison his food, clothing and shelter were, however minimally, provided and relief could be sent to his family. Once he was released he was lucky if he could return to normal civilian life and to wage-earning employment. Too often he, his wife and family could find themselves in a situation in which his freedom might mean only the freedom to starve. Thus Amnesty has always found itself faced with the dilemma of having to judge how far it could allow itself to become the far-reaching relief organization towards which its work for prisoners could easily take it, and how far it must, however unwillingly, decide to accept a more limited role.

The argument over the 'marginal' prisoner of conscience has however, centred mainly around one category in particular, that is the man who is in prison not only because of the opinions he holds but also because he has used or advocated the use of violence to make those opinions prevail.

It has been argued – never more fiercely than in the decade of the sixties and, perhaps, among those who had seen little at first hand of the results of civil or international wars – that all organized societies are at bottom violent and that therefore it is a duty not only to challenge them so as to make them reveal their violent nature, but also to use revolutionary violence to overthrow entrenched institutional violence. On these grounds, it has frequently been said that men who use violence in order to replace a corrupt society by one which they conscientiously hold to be a better one, should, if they are subsequently imprisoned, be regarded also as prisoners of conscience.

Nevertheless, this argument has been firmly rejected, partly on pragmatic and partly on theoretical grounds. In practice governments would find it only too easy to dismiss Amnesty's

124

pleas for a prisoner who openly advocated violence, and would take them as evidence that Amnesty supported subversive activities. If, on the other hand, the work is confined to those who have not taken part in violent action, it is easier to focus attention on the fact that they have been imprisoned only because of their opinions, and it is easier therefore to argue that such imprisonment is in contravention of at least the spirit of the internationally recognized Universal Declaration. It can also be said that the purpose of work for prisoners of conscience is to emphasize that rational argument should not be fettered and that since human beings are rational they should be treated with dignity: it is therefore important to oppose the use of violence since violence itself is the negation of reason.[3] (Moreover suspected violence on the part of a prisoner is often held to be sufficient justification for the use of violence against him.)

After the prisoner who is prepared to use violence, the most difficult of the marginal categories to decide upon has been that at the opposite pole – the conscientious objector in all his varieties. Since he is, by definition, opposed to violence, his imprisonment, where he has imprisoned, made him prima facie an obvious candidate for adoption as a prisoner of conscience. In fact, this area so obviously fell within Amnesty's concern that from the beginning it made a substantial contribution to the discussions of the Council of Europe which eventually led to the Council's approval of Resolution 337 in which it urged all its member countries to make legal provision for the recognition of Conscientious Objectors.

However, within this broad category there is considerable variety of individual interpretation and it soon became necessary to decide whether the term 'prisoner of conscience' applied with equal force to one who was denied by his country the opportunity of stating his position and one who had stated his position, had been offered an alternative form of service and had refused to accept the offer.[4] Perhaps the clearest issue was that of the 'selective objector'. This, at the present time, is the young man, usually in the USA or in Australia, who has declared that, while not necessarily claiming that he would not under any circumstances take up military service, he will refuse to allow himself to be conscripted for military duties in Vietnam, holding that the war in that country is an unjustifiable war.

There has, in fact, been no doubt that such a man could legitimately claim to be fulfilling a duty laid upon him by the Nuremberg Principles, which were drawn up by the International Law Commission at the request of the General Assembly of the United Nations in the light of the proceedings of the Nuremberg Tribunal. These state quite clearly that the individual's responsibility for his own acts is not expunged by government order:

'PRINCIPLE I I I
The fact that a person who committed an act which constitutes a crime under international law as Head of State or as a responsible government official does not relieve him from responsibility under international law.

PRINCIPLE I V
The fact that a person who acted pursuant to an order of his government or of a superior does not relieve him from responsibility under international law, provided a moral choice was in fact open to him.'

This review of the steps by which the limits of the term prisoner of conscience have come to be defined is intended to demonstrate the way in which the work undertaken on his behalf has become more intricate. It should not, however, obscure the fact that there are scores of categories and thousands of men and women about whose adoption there has never been any doubt.

The second reason for the success of the work was said to be the extraordinary pertinacity and resourcefulness with which it was undertaken. The original scheme was to organize ordinary men and women to work on behalf of other ordinary men and women. In an age when there was a general hopelessness about what the citizen could do to affect the policies of his own or other governments there was the determination to demonstrate that, given time, few governments could fail to respond to an appeal on behalf of the unknown made by the unknown, not on account of ideological partisanship, but simply and solely on behalf of their common humanity. Central to this was the principal of impartiality. It had to be made clear beyond all question that work for prisoners of conscience was undertaken without political or religious bias. Hence arose the concept of the 'Threes Group': this proposed that supporters should be brought

126

together into small working groups which undertook to negotiate on behalf of three prisoners simultaneously. One prisoner was to be drawn from the list of those known to be imprisoned in countries east of the Iron Curtain, one from countries to the west of it and one from the 'uncommitted' countries of Asia and Africa. The phraseology was of its time. Amnesty was launched, as has been said, in 1960. The passing of a decade, however, while it may have weakened the ideological polarization, has done little to undermine the value of this division as a practical means of establishing a balance in Amnesty's work.

There is, as it happens, one area in which such a tripartite approach would have been unusable – the Middle East, where the real opposition is between the Arab and Jewish branches of the Semitic race and where the East-West or even the so-called North-South conflicts are of only marginal importance. In working, therefore, for Jews (and others) imprisoned in Arab countries and for Arabs imprisoned in Israel, it has been essential to underline the fact that, as far as possible, both operations have been conducted simultaneously – a task which has been the more difficult to fulfil insofar as a condition of success has often been that negotiations should be carried out in confidence.

It is at this point that some central co-ordination and direction of the work has been necessary. A Secretariat and a Research Department responsible to an elected and international Executive Committee has carried out the dual task of, on the one hand, supplying the voluntary workers with information about prisoners and, on the other, of undertaking direct negotiations with governments where it seemed that a direct approach would yield the best results. Not that these are two independent operations; clearly they supplement one another and publicity – or even the suggestion of publicity – given to the murkier processes of a government is sometimes a powerful factor in encouraging it to take part in private negotiations which may lead to the release of a prisoner or to an improvement of his conditions.

It is, of course, true that some of the 'tougher-minded' governments are prepared to defy both world opinion and the reasoned humanity of an appeal by Amnesty; but such countries are few in number and so far as they are concerned, a change of attitude has to depend on the passage of time. A situation which in some respects is more difficult to deal with is that where a government shows complete readiness to talk ... and to go on talking until the question arises whether talk is a substitute for action, and negotiation merely a sophisticated method of procrastination; whether, in fact, the government has realized that Amnesty would be unwilling to conduct a large scale publicity campaign while the matters at issue were under discussion and is trading on this unwillingness to avoid having to move at all.

Despite the difficulties, however, there is no doubt that the method devised has proved its value in the long list of individuals who have been adopted as prisoners of conscience and who 'happen' to have been released subsequently. The happiest story concerns a Communist country where it was not until officials began receiving letters from Amnesty groups that they realized how many prisoners they had in their gaols and, all credit to them, then set about the situation with the result that in the end very many were released.

This brief account of the effectiveness with which international public opinion can be focused, leads to the third reason for such success as has been achieved in the work for prisoners of conscience, that is the development of an embryonic but undeniable 'international public conscience'. That some rules, however rudimentary, should govern the relations between governments has never been in doubt. What has been much slower to emerge has been the realization first that governments might be answerable to one another for the way in which they treat their own citizens and, secondly, that the citizens themselves might have duties which they could legitimately claim transcend the loyalty they owed to their own governments – in other words, that the individual might legitimately be the subject of international law.

It might be argued that such recognition had already been conceded by the Geneva conventions governing the conduct of war, but these (and their predecessors, the Hague conventions) were concerned with the way in which governments treated combatant individuals of the opposing sides. It was the experience of the Nazi and Fascist régimes culminating in the evidence produced at the Nuremberg Tribunal which made it at last possible to declare that the way in which a government – and its officials acting under its direction – treated its citizens might be a matter on which international opinion could pass judgement in the name of 'the conscience of mankind'.[5] Thus, while the notorious 'domestic jurisdiction' clause of the Charter can be – and in some situations has been – brought into use to prevent further international enquiry into the domestic operations of a government, the doctrine of the unquestioned and unquestionable sovereignty of the state has in others been under steady and successful attack. The most outstanding success has undoubtedly been that represented by the European Convention of Human Rights under an Optional Clause of which a government can allow an appellant who has unsuccessfully exhausted the appeal procedures of his own country to go beyond the final domestic court of appeal to the European Court of Human Rights at Strasbourg. Not every such appeal is accepted as valid, but it has been significant that few of those which have been accepted have had to make the full journey to the point at which the Court makes a recommendation to the Council of Ministers. Several for instance have been resolved by the appellant's government modifying its laws in such a way as to avoid the adverse comment which pursuit of the appeal would obviously have drawn on them.

Since the nineteenth century it has been rare for one state to attempt to intervene in the affairs of another on behalf of one group of that state's citizens. Where there has been such intervention, its overt concern has been only too clearly a thin disguise for its scheme for political and often territorial aggrandizement. The appeals procedure of the European Court of Human Rights is, therefore, a significant development not only in that, unlike, for instance the International Court of Justice at the Hague, it is concerned with individuals as appellants rather than states, but in that it allows for the expression of an international concern which is genuinely humanitarian and juristic in a way which does not pose a threat to the integrity of any nation involved.

The recognition of an international responsibility towards individuals carries with it, as a corollary, that there must be a responsibility of individuals towards the international community itself and those standards of public morality which have received international approval. This view was deliberately set out in the course of the Nuremberg Tribunal:

'It was submitted that international law is concerned with the actions of sovereign states and provides no punishment for individuals ... these contentions must be rejected ... Crimes against international law are committed by men, not by abstract entities, and only by punishing individuals who commit such crimes can the provisions of international law be enforced.'[6]

The consequences of this doctrine for military discipline have still to be fully spelled out, but there is no doubt that it reflects the growing awareness of the fact that a common humanity imposes a common morality.

The work for prisoners of conscience, therefore, is the crystallization of a significant development of international morality. In one sense it completes a trinity. The Red Cross acting under the Geneva Conventions is primarily concerned with those individuals who deliberately or unwittingly have been caught up in military operations; the International Commission of Jurists concerns itself not so much with individuals as such as with the Rule of Law and with elaborating and maintaining standards of legal ethics. Between the two stands Amnesty International taking as the focus of its work the individual, who has often been treated as a subversive by his government but denied the protection of the Geneva conventions, and concerning itself with law only insofar as it has borne unjustly on the man concerned.

Any such scheme, however, would be patently incomplete. Work for prisoners of conscience has thrown up many more problems than it can justifiably set itself to solve and there is a clear need for more organizations engaging in related fields – in the conditions under which prisoners are held in gaol, in the widespread use of torture, in the relief of those who have been released, but under conditions which make even the maintenance of life itself precarious for the exprisoner himself and dangerous for those of his compatriots who would help him. There is also the plight, not so much of individuals as of racial minorities often faced with persecution if not extinction ...[7] the tally could be lengthened; it is sufficient to demonstrate that, among many other crying needs, the defence and support of those citizens whose sufferings are the result of deliberate and unwarranted attacks by their governments on rights which

130

have been internationally recognized is one which mankind cannot, and fortunately is not willing, to ignore.

References

1 Given that this chapter bears the more general title of 'Prisoners of Conscience' some explanation must be offered for the constant reference to one organization in particular, Amnesty International. This is not due to any assumption that Amnesty is the only organization working effectively in this field; such an assumption would be presumptuous and arrogant. It is, rather, that it is an organization which has, from the beginning, set itself to work for men and women who are imprisoned for their opinions whatever those opinions may be. It is the denial of a basic human freedom, not support for a particular political, religious or social opinion which has formed the basis of its work.

2 *Article 18:* Everyone has the right to freedom of thought, conscience and religion; this right includes the right to change his religion or belief and freedom either alone or in community with others and in public or private, to manifest his religion or belief in teaching, practice, worship or observance.
   Article 19: Everyone has the right to freedom of opinion and expression; this right includes the freedom to hold opinions without interference and to seek, receive and impart information and ideas through any media and regardless of frontiers.

3 The exclusion of those who have used or advocated violence from adoption as prisoners of conscience has been written into the objects of Amnesty International which are given in full as follows:
   a to ensure for every person the right freely to hold and express his convictions and the obligation on every person to extend alike freedom to others; and in pursuance of that object to secure throughout the world the observance of the provisions of Articles 5, 9, 18 and 19 of the Universal Declaration of Human Rights.
   b Irrespective of political considerations, to work for the release of and provide assistance to persons who in violation of the aforesaid provisions are imprisoned, detained, restricted or otherwise subjected to physical coercion or restraint by reason of their political, religious or other

131

conscientiously held belief or by reason of their ethnic origin, colour or language, provided that they have not used or advocated violence (hereinafter referred to as 'Prisoners of Conscience').

4 In order to guide the Secretariat of Amnesty in deciding whether a Conscientious Objector may be properly adopted as a prisoner of conscience, a series of Rules was formulated and agreed at the Council meeting in Lysebu, Oslo, in 1970. These Rules were the outcome of discussion among those holding a variety of views on this subject and, naturally, go further than some, though not as far as others would personally approve of.

5 Hartley Shawcross in his speech as Chief Prosecutor at Nuremberg spoke as follows:

'Normally international law conceded that it is for the state to decide how it shall treat its own nationals; it is a matter of domestic jurisdiction. And although the Social and Economic Council of the U.N. ... does recognize that general position, yet international law in the past has made some claim that there is a limit to the omnipotence of the State, and that the individual human being, the ultimate unit of all law, is not disentitled to the protection of mankind when the State tramples on his rights in a manner which outrages the conscience of mankind.'

(Quoted by Egon Schwelb in 'Crimes against Humanity', *British Yearbook of International Law*, 1946, pp. 198-9).

6 Judgement of the International Military Tribunal ... Nuremberg, 30 September and 1 October 1946.

7 It is worth noting that Amnesty has entered into many of these fields although they could command only a marginal proportion of its time (e.g. the evidence it submitted to the UN congress at Kyoto on the treatment of prisoners in 1970). The topic to which it has devoted more than a marginal share of its time and effort is that of torture since, if torture is employed, prisoners of conscience are so often the first to suffer. In fact, the UN Declaration of Human Rights (Article 5) prohibits the use of 'torture ... cruel, inhuman or degrading treatment or punishment' and has, in its entirety been written into the Objects of Amnesty (see Note 3 above).

The international arms race
Robin Clarke

Few of us approve of violence, even if we approve the social
changes it is designed to produce. Still fewer approve of that
highly organized form of collective violence known as war. In
this chapter I want to consider a closely related problem to
which as yet no one has found a way in: the technical arms
race. The dangers of this race are usually presented as a chain
of events likely to lead to our extinction in a nuclear holocaust.
The arms race, it is argued, could propel us all towards a
nuclear suicide. I have no quarrel with this view and I believe
it to be essentially correct. But, over and above this, there is a
deeper and in some ways equally alarming situation which will
prevail whatever the outcome of the arms race. By this I mean
that the problem does not disappear if we manage in some way
to avoid World War III – either because nuclear deterrence
works as planned or, more likely, because our political leaders
manage to avoid the insane steps that would precipitate a global
nuclear war. The technical arms race, simply because it is there,
is changing us all. It is dictating the form of our economic
system, our priorities in scientific research, our personal approach to our future and the basic constructs of government.
In short, even without war, it means that we are passing our
lives within a Warfare State.

This hypothesis has an important corollary. Since the technical arms race is mainly confined to a handful of highly developed countries, it dictates their relationship to that less fortunate half of the globe which is broadly south of the equator. In the last analysis, the help we can afford to the less developed world is determined by the military preoccupations of the rich nuclear nations; and their military commitments are in fact preventing help from being given. As a result, the seeds of violence are being sown all over the globe. From South America, from Nigeria and the Congo, from the Far East and the Near East, we can see the signs of a veritable explosion of discontent, all traceable – directly or indirectly – to the gap that separates the privileged from the under-privileged.

The technical arms race, in its modern form, was conceived in the 1940s in the Allies' Manhattan project of building the atomic bomb. This project, the most outrageously successful technological endeavour ever attempted, only actually produced three bombs; but within days of two of them being exploded over Japan, the war had come to an end. Or so it seemed at the time. What actually happened was more complex.

If Hiroshima and Nagasaki mark the end of World War II, they also mark the beginning of the Cold War. The Allies' bomb was built without Soviet help – or even knowledge – and the first concern after the war was to prevent the birth of a Soviet bomb. It was really a lost cause before it started. Whatever help may have been given to the Soviet Union by espionage, the Russians already knew the most important fact: that nature had no rules which made nuclear weapons impossible. Armed with that fact, it was only a matter of time before the Soviet technical effort cracked the same problem which had beset the Manhattan effort. When they did, on 23 September 1949, a new era in military relations was born. Something close to hysteria set in among the Americans. Its cause was entirely novel; for in the autumn of 1949 there was no question of what we would now call nuclear parity. The Russians had no more than a handful of bombs compared to the thousands that were being churned off the gigantic production factories of the US nuclear effort. Why, then, were the Americans so upset?

The reason was that, for the first time in history, military power ceased to be measured in terms of weapons. Almost overnight the key factor in military planning became *technical knowledge*. It was realized that the country that held the globe in its power was the one that had pushed farthest ahead down the avenues – some might argue cul-de-sacs – of scientific research and military technology. Thus was born the US decision to make the hydrogen bomb and take that extra leap ahead. Thus was born the Soviet decision to do likewise and explode its first thermonuclear device, this time only nine months after the Americans. And thus was born a technical arms race, now more than 25 years old, which has progressively cost more money, more men and brains as every year has gone by.

This is not a weapons race in the conventional sense: it is, in fact, a knowledge race which dictates that every technically new area be explored at maximum speed, almost regardless of its possible consequences. Since no one can predict what comes out of scientific research, the military can afford to neglect no single area of investigation – they must support research on every scientific frontier. And they do not complain if the research does not lead directly to military advances. They have placed their money in a military insurance policy which, if it does not mature for one side, will not mature for the other. But we should not delude ourselves as to just how extensive the military hold on science has become. First, let us look at the situation qualitatively.

Dr. William J. Price, one time Executive Director of the US Air Force Office of Scientific Research, is one of the best witnesses. 'The AFOSR research money,' he writes, 'is of such a magnitude and nature as to help significantly in colonizing the scientific fields of potential interest to the Air Force.'[1] 'Colonizing may be described as increasing the chance of important discovery in an area deemed to hold promise for the Air Force by "raising the temperature" of the world's scientific activity in that field.'[2] It follows that if the military support were substantial in relation to the total money spent on research, military requirements would be putting a stamp on the directions of future progress; areas deemed of potential military interest would be likely to get funded before others. This is precisely what is happening at the present time.

In 1961-2 the British government spent £379·1 millions on research and development (R and D) in the UK. Almost exactly two-thirds of that – £249·8 millions – was for 'defence' projects, which means military projects of every kind. Since then the amount has increased. In the United States, the amounts are much higher. If we include spending on space and atomic energy as having at least a major role in connexion with defence, we find in 1968 that $13·2 out of $15·0 millions for R and D went on defence and related activities. Three government departments, in other words, controlled 88 per cent of the R and D budget. The other 29 agencies received only 12 per cent between them.

The manpower statistics are equally informative. In the UK about one-quarter of the country's R and D scientists are on the defence pay-roll. In the US the figure is probably about one-third to a half, depending on whether one includes space and atomic energy as wholly or only partially 'defence'. Either way, these figures illuminate the nature of the technical arms race. For defence claims between 7 and 10 per cent of the total economy in the US and the UK. The fact that the proportion of scientists employed on defence is so high shows only one thing; defence is the most research-intensive industry of them all. In no other field of human activity is there such a concentration of scientific manpower.

One view of the arms race today was expressed in 1968 by General Curtis Le May. 'I sincerely believe', he wrote, 'any arms race with the Soviet Union would act to our benefit. I believe that we can out-invent, out-research, out-develop, out-engineer and out-produce the USSR in any area from sling shots to space weapons, and in doing so become more and more prosperous while the Soviets become progressively poorer.'[3] This view raises two related points. With the present military emphasis on scientific research, it becomes essential for governments to provide long-term, peace-time plans for scientific mobilization. By this I mean that if a technical arms race is to be waged, it has to be a continuous, permanent affair which is not responsive to sudden changes in the international climate. It takes a long time to train a scientist and if his work is required for defence activities in ten years time, he will have to be put on the scientific road now. Viewed in this light the expansion of the universities over the past two decades takes on a different light. To be sure, there is value in education; but one must doubt whether that expansion would have been so swift, or whether it would have captured so high a proportion of government funds, had the only products of the universities been men of culture and learning.

The other issue raised by General Le May is that the technical arms race is also a form of economic warfare. But I suspect the General is optimistic in thinking that it will make only the Soviet Union the poorer. The blunt fact is that the arms race makes the whole world poorer. For proof one need only cite the US Arms Control and Disarmament Agency: 'Global military expenditures', it claims, 'are equivalent to the total annual income produced by the one billion people living in Latin America, South Asia and the Near East. They are greater by 40 per cent than world-wide expenditures on education by all levels of government, and more than three times world-wide expenditure on health.'[4] But what exactly is it that this enormous scientific task force aims to achieve? And what is the effect on other areas of human activity? I have already said that the arms race is not a weapons race. Indeed, over the past 15 years the number of aircraft carriers has dropped from 130 to 75 and the number of submarines from 900 to 700. But the performance of most weapons has increased dramatically. What the arms race is really about, in fact, is product improvement. Economists at the Stockholm International Peace Research Institute have tried to measure the rate of product improvement over time by reference to the cost of a weapon system. An air force fighter, for instance, cost around $110 000 in 1945 but now comes out at nearer $6·8 millions. After analysing seven such weapon systems, the SIPRI team concluded: 'The figures for the seven weapons ... suggest an average increase in performance of something over 10 per cent a year. This implies a doubling every seven years, and a twenty-fold increase over thirty years. Civil goods do not increase in performance or capability in this way ... If calculations were made on the same basis ... for a typical collection of consumer goods, they would show very little rise at all.'[5]

The SIPRI team went on to study just how research-intensive is the military industry. They found that the research input in the military field was at least 12 times greater than in civilian industry. In the UK, for instance, during 1964 $62·2 were spent on R and D for every $100 of military equipment actually bought. In civilian industry as a whole, a mere $4·9 was spent on R and D for every $100 of manufacturing output.

These figures raise a series of doubts about the wisdom of our research priorities. And they bring sudden poignancy to the famous question posed by the US nuclear physicist, Ralph Lapp. 'Who knows', he asks, 'what constructive works of science and technology might have been achieved for the benefit of mankind if the arrow of our effort had been directed towards peaceful goals?'[6]

Let us take a specific example. The world's oceans, comprising more than two-thirds of the earth's surface, have been described as our 'last resource'. They contain abundant quantities of badly needed protein food in the form of marine life. They conceal incredible reservoirs of minerals, petroleum and natural gas. They constitute, in short, a kind of natural biological factory which daily churns out all the basic materials of human life in enormous quantities. But how to get at it? Until, say, a decade ago the ocean environment remained an unknown quantity. Men had skimmed its surface but had never risen to the major challenge of exploring and exploiting a totally new environment in the way in which they had earlier leapt at the challenge of exploring space.

By the late 1960s things had begun to change. A major oceanographic research programme was begun by a small group of countries – mainly the nuclear powers. The reason was not hard to find. Nuclear deterrents, through constant product improvement, were in danger of being blasted off the face of the Earth by enemy missiles. The only long-term answer looked like concealing nuclear missiles beneath the ocean surface where they could be neither found nor destroyed. And so the oceanographic research bill began to rise very fast. Those who have watched this trend over the past five years may have been given the impression – quite deliberately — that this programme had to do with marine food and minerals. The sad fact is that these objectives were of secondary importance. In 1970, for instance, US funds for ocean research reached $528 millions. Of that, the US Navy controlled $298 millions directly and a great deal more indirectly.

The Navy claimed that its aims were altruistic. Talking of the new fleet of underwater craft that had been developed for ocean-ography, one Navy biologist wrote in 1965: 'The ultimate aim is to exploit the ocean's vast resources of proteins and minerals.'[7] Many similar claims by Navy writers could be annotated by anyone wanting to plough through the literature. But what the US Navy says in public and what it says in private are different things. Thus Robert H. Baldwin, Under-Secretary of the US Navy, told a private conference on 11 January 1966: 'We are involved in deep ocean engineering because it contributes to our assigned missions; we are not in the business of exploiting the ocean's abundant mineral or living resources.'[8] This means that our knowledge of the ocean is being acquired in a lop-sided way. There are two main results. First, the dangers of the arms race are being extended into a completely new environment, with all the potential for vast financial waste which that entails. Second, those countries in dire need of fish protein as food must wait yet longer while the nuclear powers work out their sub-oceanographic nuclear fixations.

Wisdom has been in pretty short supply when one considers some of the other technical adventures of the 1960s. Take the grandest adventure of all, the exploration of space. Cut through the public relations exercise which has obscured the real meaning of this exercise, and go back a decade to when the US decision to put a man on the moon was imminent. This is the brief received by President Kennedy from the Administrator of NASA, James Webb, and from Robert McNamara, Defence Secretary: 'Our attainments in space are a major element in the international competition between the Soviet system and our own. The non-military, non-commercial and non-scientific but "civilian" projects such as lunar and planetary exploration are, in this sense, part of the battle along the fluid front of the cold war.'[9]

One could, of course, go on to outline all the ways in which the Apollo programme to land a man on the moon, and its associated activities, have served military purposes rather than civilian, scientific or even commercial ends. But let us instead accept the conclusion of three independent investigators who, after lengthy research, published their own account of the space programme: 'The builders of Apollo,' they concluded, 'were not technicians at work in a laboratory insulated from the world. They were soldiers in an age when technology has become warfare by other means.'[10]

There could be no clearer indication than this of the yawning gap that separates the public image of the space programme from its real one. NASA, like the US Navy, has for ten years led us up a garden path, allegedly flanked by the beautiful flowers of science and human adventure. The garden path in fact leads to a new battle front by way of those characteristic acronyms of the 1970s, ABM and MIRV.

The technical arms race is now entering a new, more costly and yet more perilous phase. That it can now do so is due mainly to the antics of our space pioneers over the previous decade. They have shown the way to a deeper understanding of rocket propulsion, of atmospheric re-entry, of space navigation and dynamics. From these advances stems the possibility of designing missiles to destroy other missiles (ABMs) and of fitting each missile with up to 14 separately manoeuvrable nuclear warheads (MIRVs). Today a US citizen faces the prospect that his government will shortly invest more than $10,000 millions in an ABM system to protect, not his cities, but his own missiles and their command posts. He knows that his government is planning through MIRVs to increase the total number of US nuclear warheads from 2382 to between 7000 and 10000. The inevitable Soviet response will follow. He knows, too, that neither of these developments will make him richer and that both will make his future less likely. For the technical arms race is a race that cannot be won; its competitors are all losers, and they all know it when they take up their positions at the starting line. Should there be any remaining doubt about this, let me quote, not a critic of the US defence effort, but one of its ex-directors of Defence Research and Engineering, Dr. Herbert York. In 1969 he wrote: '... the ABM issue is a particularly clear example of the futility of searching for technical solutions to what is essentially a political problem, namely the problem of national security. The arms race is not so much a series of political provocations followed by hot emotional reactions as it is a series of technical challenges followed by cool, calculated responses in the form of ever more costly, more complex and more fully developed automatic devices .... Thus the steady advance of arms technology may not be leading us to the ultimate wea-

140

pon but rather to the ultimate absurdity: a completely automatic system for deciding whether or not doomsday has arrived.'[11]

With this picture of the arms race in mind, I want now to return to the principle theme of this book: what can any of us, as ordinary citizens, do about it? The question is hideously difficult. This is not a simple question of interfering with or influencing the normal political processes. As I have stressed, what we are involved in is a technical arms race and not a weapons race in the conventional sense. The race is being run in the laboratories in terms of differential equations, solid state reactions, mass spectroscopy, 'scattering effects' and all the other jargon of our scientific age. And so the first reaction of even the educated layman is one of despair. How can he possibly have any effect on, or even make any contribution to, a field which he cannot begin to understand?

At least the answer to that one is simple. We can all understand enough of what is going on to appreciate its essential character. We must not be frightened of the technical nature of the modern arms race, or the fog of jargon issued by experts in the field when they discuss their work. To claim that only those with years of research experience are qualified to discuss technological research is humbug and we should recognize it as such. As a practical aid to the recognition of future humbugs, let me give an example.

Today's deterrence theory is vastly complicated and becoming more so. For a learned discussion of it, one would need to have command of scores of technical concepts such as 'first strike', 'counter-force strike', 'penetration aids', 'parity', 'acceptable minimum damage', 'yield ratios', 'delivery accuracy', 'megatonnage equivalents' and many other terms. The job of the critic is not to spend a couple of years in a library following through the implications of these technical terms. It is, instead, to penetrate to the heart of the matter; and in the case of deterrence, that has been aptly summarized for us by Theodore Roszak. 'Deterrence', he writes, 'is no more than an exquisitely rationalized social commitment to the practice of genocide.'[12] The question before us is whether we wish our governments, in our name, to commit us to this practice. If we don't, then the whole creaking edifice of that branch of learning known as 'nuclear strategy' is demolished at one blow. With it, I should add, will come the destruction of a substantial part of our scientific and technical effort as practised in the nuclear countries.

It is important to learn to differentiate scientific work performed for civil ends from research which has a primary military objective. The ocean and space examples I have mentioned are sufficient to show that the real objects of a good deal of scientific research are rarely apparent. Sometimes they are deliberately obscured and sometimes they become unintentionally veiled by scientists who simply believe they are carrying out the kind of research they wish to pursue; and the fact that their research money comes from the Pentagon or the Ministry of Defence is an accident caused by the somewhat curious structure of contemporary society. Here, too, some humbug recognition is in order. Neither the Pentagon nor the Ministry of Defence spends money without a military objective in mind. To be sure, that objective may be extremely diffuse, but its essential characteristic must be recognized if we are to understand the nature of the driving force behind the technical arms race.

Articles are published in the scientific journals by authors who describe the secondary, civilian objectives of their research in glowing terms, the whole package being dressed up as one of those vital contributions to the future welfare of mankind which merits an immediate doubling of research funds. Not until too late may the editor discover that the author's funds come from the Pentagon and that the primary objective of the research was actually to provide a new series of building blocks for the next round of the arms race. We have all read articles of this kind in magazines and the newspapers and it is not that difficult to separate what is essentially military research from civilian, providing one is prepared to read between the lines. I urge everyone who spots this kind of deception to write to the editor concerned, insisting that the record be put straight and that the real objectives of the research be described at equal length.

But writing to an editor or two can hardly affect the race to oblivion on which we are now engaged. It falls almost infinitely short of what is needed. Yet it does lead on to a number of ideas which I believe must gain general acceptance if the arms race is ever to be halted.

Many people see the arms race as simply a part of the struggle for power between the vital political camps known as 'capitalism' and 'communism'. Solve that battle, this argument would run, and the arms race will simply disappear. I think that this view is profoundly mistaken. I suspect that the arms race has nothing to do with left and right, or with any other of the conventional measures of political belief. It comes, I believe, from a society in which there will always be internal dissensions, and which has come to believe that the advancement of scientific knowledge is a sacrosanct principle on which all human progress depends. The inevitable result is that the dissenting factions grow suspicious that the knowledge they create may be used against them. Yet why do we have to accept this technological imperative? If such high proportions of our science and technology are used for military ends, it would obviously be a safer world if there were less science and technology.

Why this view, in 1970, should still be regarded as heresy I am unable to explain. Yet it is. Any suggestion that research in any area should be slowed down or stopped because it might lead to undesirable consequences is always greeted by shrieks of protest and the implication that we are once again to be plunged back into the Dark Ages when learning was suppressed. Few are bold enough to point out that an age in which 'overkill' has become a subject for a Ph.D. thesis and 'nuclear strategy' an accepted part of a university curriculum is already a dark one. The idea that science must go on, whatever the cost, is not an inviolable principle. Why the collections of individuals that comprise society cannot reach the same rational conclusion is one of the great mysteries of the twentieth century. To put it more paradoxically, it is one of the most widely held 'unscientific' myths of our time.

Ultimately, then, I would suggest that the most constructive approach to the arms race is currently to ponder this paradox. This is not a practical recommendation but a theoretical one. It may be, however, that it is our theory that is at fault – in which case time is needed to produce the seed bed of ideas from which practical action can spring. As an aid to the process, let me conclude with a return, not quite to the Dark Ages, but to a time much closer to them than now.

Some 300 years ago Leonardo da Vinci invented the submarine. He later wrote in his notebooks that he deliberately suppressed knowledge of this invention 'on account of the evil nature of men, who would practice assassination at the bottom of the sea'.[13] How right he was and how wrong we have been to assume that the accumulation of new knowledge is worth *any* cost. When that cost becomes the survival of the human race, the proposition is surely one that should be questioned.

References

1 Price, William J., *The Role of A F O S R in A F O S R Research*. Arlington, Virginia. A F O S R 67 – 0300.

2 Price, William J., Ashley, William G., and Martino, Joseph P., *Relating the Accomplishments of A F O S R to the Needs of the Air Force*. Arlington, Virginia. A F O S R 66 – 2423.

3 Le May, Curtis E., with Smith, Dale O. (1968), *America is in Danger*. Funk and Wagnall, New York.

4 U S Arms Control and Disarmament Agency (1968), *World Military Expenditures, 1966–67*. Research Report 66-52. Washington D C.

5 *S I P R I Yearbook on World Armaments and Disarmament 1968-69* (1969). Duckworth, London.

6 Lapp, Ralph (1963), *Kill and Overkill*. Weidenfeld and Nicholson, London.

7 Recknitzer, Andreas (1965), Underwater Exploration. *Science Journal, 1*, 8.

8 Quoted in Hersch, Seymour M. (1968), *An Arms Race on the Sea Bed?* War/Peace Report (August – September 1968).

9 Quoted in Young, Hugo, Silcock, Bryan, and Dunn, Peter (1969), *Journey to Tranquillity*. Cape, London.

10 Young, Hugo, Silcock, Bryan, and Dunn, Peter (1969), *Journey to Tranquillity*. Cape, London.

11 York, Herbert (1969), Military Technology and National Security. *Scientific American, 221*, 2.

12 Roszak, Theodore (1970), *The Making of a Counter Culture*. Faber and Faber, London.

13 Quoted in Mumford, Lewis (1967), *The Myth of the Machine*. Secker and Warburg, London.

The containment of conflict

Geoffrey Vickers

1 Conflict and co-operation

The continuance of human life on acceptable terms – perhaps on any terms – clearly depends on our learning to contain and resolve conflict *and* to develop co-operation at levels far beyond those yet attained by men and perhaps beyond their inherent capacities. So the words conflict and co-operation have come to stand for opposites, each charged with strong emotional and moral overtones. Both the antithesis and the attitudes are natural but they over-simplify the situation.

Conflict is more than the absence of co-operation, co-operation more than the absence of conflict. Conflictual situations are typified by the 'zero-sum game', where the gain of one is necessarily the corresponding loss of the other – the relation, for example, of two sides on a football field. The co-operative situation is typified by the common enterprise, where each depends on all the others to achieve what each desires and none can achieve alone – the relation, for example, which exists between the members of each team. Conflictual and co-operative situations can and usually do co-exist; there are few, if any, conflictual situations involving no interest which the contestants have in common; few if any co-operative situations involving no conflict between the parties. Both types of situation can exist in varying degrees of intensity, diminishing to a common vanishing point – ever less attainable – where each party can go his way, unhindering and unhelping, unhindered and un-helped.

Furthermore, both words, in different contexts, have different connotations which are hard to reconcile. Conflict, in various forms, plays a constructive part in the regulation of human, no less than non-human societies. Legal procedures and electoral procedures – both 'zero-sum games' – are ritualized forms of conflict which are highly prized as social and political regula-tors. And though co-operation carries an aura of social approval, compromise, which it often involves, is an ambivalent, if not a dirty word. The man prepared to fight and even die – or more significantly kill – for his 'principles' is an admired type, especi-ally in Western societies.

The tangle of meanings and attitudes associated with con-flict and co-operation is evidently more complex than at first appears; so I will approach it through two other terms which are less highly charged. Organization necessarily involves *con-straint* and is equally necessary for *enablement*.

Every organization is both more and less than the sum of its parts. It is less, because each of its constituents is necessarily constrained by the mere fact of being included in a wider organization; some of its potentialities cannot be realized within the limitations which that organization imposes. On the other hand, an organization is also necessarily more than the sum of its constituents, because its organized constituents can do what none of them could do alone – often including the ability to survive. So constraint is endemic in every organiza-tion and so is enablement; and the greater the enablement achieved, the greater the price which must be paid in con-straint and therefore in potential conflict.

Since our world consists of a bewildering variety of organiza-tions, which are themselves parts of larger organizations, some overlapping, some hierarchically structured, we can see that the definitions with which I began are inadequate, since they imply conflict and co-operation between units of the same kind. We are all familiar with conflict not only between one indi-vidual and another but also between individuals and the organ-izations which comprise them, especially their political institutions; between different levels and divisions of an organ-

146

ization; and between organizations, reaching their extreme in clashes between 'independent' nation states. These different types of conflict need some separate consideration, but it is my present object to distinguish what can be usefully said of all of them.

2 The meaning of containment

A further difficulty needs to be resolved. Two of the many senses in which we use the word conflict need to be distinguished at the outset, because they are essential to the subject of this paper, the *containment* of conflict. Conflicts of interest, view or valuation constantly arise and are as constantly resolved or contained, without resort to those forms of attempted coercion or mutual destruction which we sometimes distinguish as 'conflict', using the word to denote particular forms or degrees of mutual struggle which in the context we regard as different from others in some critical way. If in any specific context we wonder whether conflict will be resolved or contained or whether it will erupt in 'conflict', we and others usually know quite clearly the threshold we have in mind. It is the threshold beyond which a conflict can only be 'fought out'. We need two words to distinguish between these two senses; but no well recognized words are available.

In international relations the threshold is typified by the transition from 'peace' to 'war'. But war would be too narrow a term to cover all conflict which lies beyond the threshold. Sometimes it is indeed marked by the eruption of physical violence, sometimes by the transition from legal to illegal methods; but it is wider even than these indices. I will describe the crossing of the threshold as breakdown, because it involves breakdown of accepted ways of containing or resolving conflict. Subjectively, it means that some or all the parties involved have suspended or withdrawn their willingness to be bound by these accepted ways. They have redefined the 'other' as enemy or at least alien – as a part of their environment to which they owe no duty. Objectively, it means the breakdown of the system which these ways help to regulate. The subjective and the objective thresholds are not the same but to cross either is likely to involve crossing the other.

This distinction implies a definition of peace which seems to me to be relevant to this book. Those who work for 'peace' at any level of conflict, international, national or individual, want if they can to 'resolve' conflict, to conjure it away; but they have an equally real and sometimes more realistic goal, the goal of containing it within both the subjective and the objective thresholds which I have described and which, for simplicity, I will treat as one, except where I need to distinguish between them, as I shall do in the last section of this paper.

This is the threshold with which I am concerned; and I am particularly concerned with national thresholds, by which I mean, the thresholds of the system whose main political regulator is the central government, for me the central government of the United Kingdom. If this society – and other Western societies – is to remain viable at its present level of organization, it must, I think, learn to generate less conflict or to resolve its conflicts more completely. But both these are learning processes and learning processes take time. Unless in the meantime, conflict can be contained, the system will break down, conflict will escalate and much will be lost, perhaps irrevocably. So the containment of conflict deserves attention in its own right.

I will first describe in very summary fashion what seem to me to be the trends which have led to the present stage of instability. Then I will examine the techniques available to us for resolving or containing conflict. Finally I will consider the concept of authority and its role in the containment of conflict.

3 Social regulators for muting conflict

Constraint does not necessarily engender conflict, still less breakdown. All human societies depend on complex regulators which mute the conflicts they would otherwise engender and which resolve or contain those which emerge, as well as securing the co-operation on which they equally depend. Their main regulators are 'rule' and 'role'. A system of rules, from explicit laws to the subtlest conventions of courtesy, provides an established answer to most common conflictual situations; consider, for example, how much potential conflict is prevented from even emerging simply by the habit of queuing and the rule of the road. Within the system of rules, a more extensive and flexible system of roles distributes and legitimises powers of decision. This is made both acceptable and adaptable in so far as both rule and role prescribe and limit the range of discretion of all power-holders, by the self- and mutual expectations attached to their roles, and equally prescribe and limit the range of pressures which others may bring to bear on them. And even where conflict remains a form of regulation, it is ritualized and limited by rule and role.

The essence of this type of regulation is a system of self-expectations and mutual expectations in the minds of the members. I will refer to its product as 'the constraints and assurances of membership'. It is not the only cohesive force in a society, especially a modern Western society, but no society can exist without some measure of it. It is seen at its best in societies where this net of self- and mutual expectations is most comprehensive, well-accepted, stable and apt. The most obvious examples, perhaps, are to be found among those simple and most ancient of human traditional societies – associations of families living by food gathering and hunting, with or without some animal husbandry or simple agriculture. They may seem remote from us; but it is they which have nurtured mankind through all but the last few hundred generations, that is for more than ninety per cent of its existence as a species and which probably nurtured its pre-human ancestors for far longer; and we are not yet so successful that we can regard it as permanently outmoded.

In such societies the social dimension comprehends both the political and the personal to an extent which it is hard for us to conceive. In consequence conflict within the society is at a very low level. On the other hand, between one of these societies and another, conflict is usually endemic. The reason is obvious, though commonly ignored. Men have depended on men since men were men; they only became men and only survived as men by learning to depend on each other far more than any other creatures. They are *biologically* social creatures. But human societies have not depended on each other until very recently. Although they have been enriched by exchanges of goods, techniques and ideas made by individuals, their collective relations with each other have commonly been hostile, even mutually predatory, throughout recorded time; muted only by distance and the limitations of their free resources.

149

It does not follow that relations between societies must necessarily be hostile. We do not know the integrative capacities or limitations of the human species. Organizing forces have been at work for a few millennia to promote their co-operation and mute their conflicts at this inter-societal level also. But it remains, I believe, a fact of great importance that co-operation between human individuals has always been biologically necessary, whilst co-operation between human societies has not.

4 The limits of organization

It is a far cry from those primitive societies to our own. Human organization has grown in scale enormously, attesting the development of cohesive forces that we know too little about. The progress has not been uniform. Political empires have risen and fallen; Toynbee surveyed their awful sequence only a decade or two before the development of systems theory might have offered him new concepts with which to express his intuitions. Economic exchange has fluctuated no less. Before the sack of Mohenjo – Daro in the sixteenth century B C, a dweller in the Indus valley, as Geoffrey Bibby has estimated,[11] could have visited Norway and returned within two or three years, using only regular commercial transport routes. Three thousand years would pass before this would again be possible. Cultural exchange has fluctuated no less; a medieval scholar could pass from one European university to another in pursuit of learning far more easily in some ways than he can today. Today's ideological curtains, iron, bamboo and other, seem to me to have no historical parallel in their divisive power. But on balance the development has been towards greater integration and we can list some of the disparate causes. The accumulation and unequal distribution of wealth and power increased the coercive abilities of the strong and led to concentrations of political power, hierarchically organized. Industry and commerce created their own world-wide networks, transcending and yet ministering to the concentrations of political power and increasing the disparity of their strength. Cultural empires also waxed and waned but on balance grew greater – shared systems of language and thought which extended the 'constraints and assurances of membership' within their boundaries, sometimes even beyond them. Increasing facilities for communication served to further both integration and the rival development next to be mentioned. There emerged a dimension of organized power, governmental and extra-governmental, far transcending the early social matrix. I will call it the institutional dimension.

At the other end of the scale, there emerged, somewhat later, a personal dimension which was equally new. Western culture, atomizing society, evolved the concept of the free and 'independent' individual, authorized and bound to criticise every claim made on him and to acknowledge only those which he freely accepts. I shall not attempt here[2] to trace the history of events and ideas which has created this unique Western concept of the individual or to list the benefits, the costs and the contradictions with which it has saddled him. I seek only to summarize the broad trend which in Western societies has separated the personal level on the one hand, as well as the institutional level on the other, from the social matrix which once comprehended both.

This dichotomy is, I believe, the main reason why our contemporary societies begin to generate more conflict than they can contain.

Western societies are a vast structure of organizations, some of more than national scale. Political societies unite under detailed regulation populations which may number hundreds of millions. Even city governments regulate the affairs of tens of millions. Economic organizations employ tens, even hundreds of thousands and sometimes operate in a score of countries. Trade unions have memberships approaching a million. Even universities may comprise scores of thousands of students and faculty on a dozen campuses. Each of these organizations is a hierarchic power structure which has often far outgrown its supporting social structure and comprises manifold cultures and sub-cultures, none sufficiently comprehensive to contain or resolve the conflicts that it generates. All in consequence are in danger of losing the main sources of their legitimacy, which is the base of their self-regulating power.

Between these institutions, whether in the public or the private sector, there are developing ever stronger bonds of interdependence. These are also sources of conflict. There is conflict between the hierarchical levels of organizations, both public and private, and equally between their functional divisions. There is conflict between the public and private sectors, as each becomes more dependent on the other and more constrained to allow for and even help to implement the policies of the other. These conflicts present challenges so great that theorists of organization search intensively for alternative patterns which will reduce the level of mutual distrust and mutual frustration.

The problem is not merely one of organization. The containment of conflict (still more the mediating of co-operation) between and within these large organizations depends also on those social and cultural factors which I described earlier as the constraints and assurances of membership. The more complex and conflicting the variety of claims made by these overlapping institutions on those who control them at all levels, the more unlikely it is that these will be able to reconcile and respond to them all or to tolerate the tensions of their irreconcilable claims. In so far as these strains become too great to be borne, those subject to them will draw more narrowly the allegiances which they accept and allow conflict to polarize between the others.

But more conspicuous and more dangerous, I think, is the widening gulf which is developing between what I have called the personal and the institutional level – between individual men and *all* the institutions on which they depend.

The constraints imposed on men by organization are felt by them more sharply than its enablements; so the growth of human societies has always been limited by its members' willingness to tolerate the constraints which are its necessary price. But this tolerance has always been further restricted by another factor. Organizations, for all their usefulness, have always been the means whereby men have dominated their fellows. From the earliest dynasties of Egypt, one enduring symbol of human oppression has been the official, exercising the power of an institution by virtue of his role in it. And as such he has been feared even when he has not used his position (as he has often done) to exalt himself and his friends and to torment his enemies.

So the attitude of men towards human institutions has always been ambivalent. On the one hand, the institution is not only

152

useful but enlarging. It represents the claims of all, as against the claim of the individual, the claim of tomorrow as against today. But equally, every institution carries the inherent threat that it will pursue its own institutional interests and those of its office holders to the exclusion of those which justify its existence; and the first of these threats is even more fearful than the second. Corrupt office holders can be bribed or ousted or even held effectively and continuously responsible. But nothing can prevent them from being guided to some extent by the standards of success which govern their institution. And these are bound to be to some extent different from the personal standards of those they serve; for every system has its own coherence to guard, its own standards, legitimate as well as illegitimate, to attain, if it is to remain a viable servant of those whose needs it serves.

In Western cultures at the present time this ambivalence has reached unparalleled levels of paranoia and with good reason. These societies exist only by virtue of the enormous size and multiplicity of the economic and political organizations which they have learned to create. Yet three centuries of cultural history have taught them to distrust institutional power and to attend far more to controlling its abuse than to creating the conditions which enable it to work at all – the first of which is that trust which they increasingly withhold.

There are reasons for this crisis of confidence. The scale of human organization achieved in recent centuries, unstable though it is, should evoke astonishment; and three linked factors combine to test its weaknesses. One of these is the multiplication of human interaction, of which exploding populations is only one of many causes. Generally speaking, multiplying interaction increases the occasions for conflict, whilst making ever greater demands on co-operation. It is to be expected that a point will come where the one will defeat the other.

Among these interactions one kind demands special attention; the interaction of diverse cultures. Whilst this may conceivably, in time, produce a common culture and even (though still more improbably) a 'better', its immediate and perhaps its final effect is that each culture is eroded by the others. The effect of this is that the total volume of assured self- and mutual expectations becomes less extensive and less assured, or even

153

polarized in mutual opposition; and therewith rule and role, those basic regulators, become confused or impotent.

These challenges are compounded by rising rates of change, in the physical, the institutional and the cultural environment. Since regulation depends on shared and reliable expectations, there is a threshold beyond which changes in these expectations cannot be assimilated quickly enough to maintain their regulatory power. This threshold is passed ever more frequently.

Finally, the overcrowding of the planet poses alternatives of starker conflict or more comprehensive co-operation than ever before. The most obvious sign is the closing of the frontiers. Throughout human history until the present century there has always been somewhere to go. The adventurous, the deviant, the crowded, the rejected, the losers in fights could escape into underpopulated, unappropriated space. Today, this safety valve is almost closed. Henceforward nearly all human beings are doomed to live until death doth them part in the societies into which they are born.

5 The resolution of conflict

The heirs of the Enlightenment believed strongly in the power of reason to resolve conflict. Sharing a culture which they supposed (in so far as they were conscious of it) to be inherent in the human mind, they underrated the role played by what I have called the constraints and assurances of membership. The exercise of reason, as they understood it, can seldom, if ever *resolve* conflict without the support of some such constraints and assurances. The techniques they distinguished are none the less powerful.

Simplest of all is the bargain. In the vocabulary of classical economics bargaining is the process by which a willing but not constrained buyer and seller in a free market discover whether there are any terms on which the one will sell and the other will buy. In these idealized conditions – which have seldom existed and are even more rare today – neither can threaten the other; for by definition there are other equally willing buyers and sellers in a market which no individual can manipulate. I will generalize bargain to include the conditional offer of any benefit; and I will distinguish it sharply from threat, which is a technique of containment.

154

Some conflicts can be resolved in this way. Terms are agreed which are acceptable to both; there is no longer anything to dispute. The procedure is much more limited in scope than was once supposed. Not everything – and not everyone – has a price, even if there were a buyer able and willing to pay it. Nor will a market suffice to distribute places in the inadequate lifeboats of a sinking ship, a situation more common than economists like to suppose. None the less, bargaining (in this restricted sense) is a valid and important way of resolving conflict.

Some conflicts can be resolved by what I will call integration. Analysis of the situation as seen by each of the contestants may suggest a solution which will satisfy the requirements of each with no sacrifice by the other. Such solutions are only found by patient analysis and comparison of the contestants' views and demands and they are the simplest form of a process which I will call mutual persuasion.

A more radical and difficult kind of solution is by what I will call reinterpretation. One or all the contestants are led to change their view of the situation to one more comprehensive and less exclusive of the situation as seen by the other. With 'the situation' thus restructured, an integrative solution is often possible that was not possible before.

The way we value a situation is often given by the way we classify it; so merely to reclassify it may resolve deep differences of valuation. A riot is a riot; but to see it *also* as a protest against oppression or injustice (if this be its origin) mitigates the conflict between the rioters and the forces of law and order by making available a common universe of discourse. Many situations are radically revalued simply by being renamed. The major tactic of those who have campaigned for more human treatment of insanity has been to establish it as mental *illness* and thus entitled to the whole range of attitudes which illness has come to evoke.

A still more refined exercise in mutual persuasion is to secure revaluation even without reinterpretation. It has been done; the classic example is slavery. The definition of slavery today is as it was two thousand years ago; but our attitudes towards it have radically changed; and one agency of the change has been the advocacy of dedicated men.

The process of mutual persuasion is obscure. Parties to a

negotiation testify to their belief in it by the way they appeal to whatever standards of fact or value they suppose to be shared by the other parties. There is room for special pleading, even for deceit. Those who listen do so primarily because it is tactically important for them to know the position of their adversary as he sees it. They seldom wish to be persuaded. None the less, it is rare for this procedure to leave either party where it began. Its own view is changed, not only of the courses of action available but of the factors which should be included in its concept of the situation and even in the way these should be evaluated.

We thus use in practice a model of mutual persuasion far more sophisticated than those which theorists have put forward. For long the resolution of conflict was described in mechanical terms as a resolution of *forces*; but this serves as an approximation only to the crudest examples of resolution by violence. Later, since it became respectable to distinguish communication from transfers of energy, games theorists have usefully modelled strategies applicable to many situations common to war and business, on the assumption that the parties are inaccessible to each other's persuasion. Useful though these models are, it is well to remember their limitations. Games theory assumes that the rules of the game and therewith the definition of success will stay put at least for the duration of the game. But as all policy makers learn to their cost, both the rules of the game and the standards of success are, in the game of life, constantly being altered by the course of the game. That is what the game is about. The problems of science and technology are not typical of life's problems but limiting cases, of only instrumental use or relevance.

All the rational techniques of conflict resolution depend on some shared constraints and assurances of membership; and, more important, they are the main means by which these constraints and assurances are built up. Even bargaining is only useful when the parties have some assurance that the bargain will be kept. The techniques of mutual persuasion, in ascending order, demand willingness and ability to take the role of the other, a joint interest in avoiding 'breakdown' and some belief in the power of persuasion and therefore some willingness to be persuaded. All depend on human communication and on the shared culture and shared trust which make human communication possible. And as all experienced negotiators know, these are themselves partly the product of negotiation, patiently nursed and easily destroyed.

6 The containment of conflict

The containment of conflict is another matter. Endemic in any society is a certain amount of conflict which is experienced as such but which does not lead to breakdown because it is 'contained'. The most obvious agent of containment is simply impotence. The unsatisfied party, thwarted by other men or circumstance, has no means – or thinks he has no means – to make his will prevail or even to make his protest heard.

Impotence shades imperceptibly into the state of being deterred by threat, the most ubiquitous form of containment. Those who 'cannot' because they know they would be killed if they did, are contained not by impotence but by threat.

Threat plays an important part in nearly all negotiations – including most political demonstrations, which are communications in the ongoing negotiation of politics. The threatener promises to inflict some damage, hazard or loss unless concession is made to his view – a technique to be sharply distinguished from bargaining as defined earlier, though the two are seldom separate and often deliberately confused. They are different in their psychological working, in their character and in their effect; for failure to agree to an offer leaves things in *status quo*, whereas refusal to yield to a threat results, if the other party is in earnest, in the occurrence of whatever was threatened, and this, whatever else it does, is likely to change the *status quo*, perhaps irreversibly. It is especially important to draw the distinction, because the power of threat is increasing and is likely to go on increasing in an ever more inter-dependent society, where ever smaller groups have ever greater power to hurt ever more of their neighbours. The expression 'collective bargaining' grossly misdescribes the mutual relations of employers and employed in wage negotiations, in which one side has the power only to bargain, whilst the other can only threaten. Happily, this bare description does not adequately describe the content of that most curious relationship.

What is threatened is some form of coercion or destruction. Coercion may take many forms but it can operate in only two ways. It may make one of the contestants impotent to continue the conflict or it may induce him to contain it through the further element of threat which it usually contains. Most acts of coercion which do the first (e.g. imprisonment) do the second also.

All forms of coercion are to be distinguished from destruction. Coercion at least acknowledges that the adversary is human; for only human beings can be coerced. Today in many endemic conflicts one or both parties are committed to the destruction of the other or of something defended by the other. The object of destruction may be an individual, an office, an institution, a system, even a State or a race. There are many conflicts of this intensity in the world today; and unless and until they can be resolved, they can only be contained, unless they are to be fought out to their own intended 'ultimate solution'.

This analysis of containment reveals the dilemma inherent in containing conflict and especially conflict so intense as to aim at solution by destruction. All the techniques I have described as available for containing conflict are equally available for conducting it. To 'fight out' a conflict is the most ancient and universal way of settling it. Techniques for doing so economically and with sufficient finality are observed and admired by ethologists among stags, wolves and other species, with which human societies are often unfavourably compared.

The comparison is, I think, unfair. Human societies may be less successful but they have attempted much more. They have institutionalised the containment of conflict by a balancing act which, like all such acts, is never done once for all. One half of the act is to maintain in a central executive a sufficient concentration of coercive power to contain the conflicts which the society engenders and cannot resolve. The other half is to maintain sufficient control over the executive to prevent it from engendering more conflict than it can contain, or from stifling desired and practicable change in the name of containing conflict. Historically, the most conspicuous side of the story in the West may have been the progressive establishment of control over the executive; but the need to maintain that power has been equally constant and sometimes dominant. Fear of anarchy and fear of tyranny are equally valid regulators. Which

158

should be operative in practice depends on the situation. Like any other regulator, the threshold that gives the loudest warning is the one which at the moment is in most imminent danger of being overrun.

The role of the State in containing internal conflicts has always been ambivalent, never more than now. It is also subject to limitations inherent in its task and its tools. One of these is inherent in the definition of its task.

The essence of control over the executive is to establish agreed rules for unleashing its power. Hence the enormous importance attached by Western states to the distinction between the lawful and the unlawful. Hence also the importance attached to the *form*, rather than the *occasion* of a conflict. It is much safer to ban *ways* of waging a conflict than to suppress *kinds* of conflict. The rule of law is a precious social achievement. But it holds only so long as it is valued enough to evoke the support needed to maintain it; and this in turn depends largely on how widely acceptable are the legal ways of pursuing whatever are the major conflicts of the day.

A second limitation is inherent in the kinds of conflict which this power may be invoked to regulate. These are of three main kinds – conflicts between members; conflicts aimed at changing the law or the constitution; and conflicts aimed at changing the policies of the executive, with or without changing the actual office holders. In dealing with conflicts of the first kind, the executive may be and may be seen to be independent. In conflicts of the second kind, it is involved but only as a guardian. But in conflicts of the third kind it is itself one of the contestants. Its acceptability as a 'container' is likely to vary with its independence.

Another limitation inheres in the weapons which the executive can use. Force is of limited use in the containment of conflict. It is at its most effective in containing the conflicts of individuals. The killer, the robber, the cheat can be apprehended; and, when convicted, can be confined; and when confined, are made almost impotent to kill, to rob and to cheat. This much at least force can do; and when the power of the State is used thus, it is seen as the instrument not of the executive but of the law and is approved by those to whom the law seems just, even where they disagree about the aptness of particular penalties.

But what if the act is directed against the law itself? Or the Constitution? Or the policies or persons of the office-holders? It is then a political act; more, a political communication, amplified by the treatment which it earns as a breach of the law. It is not only a violation of order in general but a protest against a particular 'order'. And the state which prosecutes it as 'disorder' is inescapably acting as the guardian not only of order but of a particular order, of which it is a beneficiary, as well as a guardian. The fiercer the conflict on the political issue involved, the harder it is to distinguish the defence of 'law and order' from the defence of particular laws and a particular order.

Another limitation is inherent in these clumsy weapons. They are designed to constrain individuals. What if one or all the parties to the conflict are angry mobs? Even where no branch of the state is involved in the conflict itself – as in a lynching or a sectarian or racial riot – the executive cannot intervene to apprehend the individuals responsible; any arrests made can only be 'tokens'. It can only disperse the contestants by the threat or exercise of greater force. And this changes the character of its intervention. It is seen as the agent not of the law but of the executive. And what if this kind of conflict is not merely between private parties but involves the law, the constitution or the executive as objects of the conflict? Here lies the boundary of civil war.

Like the techniques of resolution, the techniques of containment cannot be safely considered in abstraction from the constraints and assurances of membership. It is these which, in the first instance, give a special meaning to impotence, by restraining contestants from using or even considering forms of attack or protest which are excluded by rule and role. It is these in the second place which rally support against contestants who ignore that restraint, irrespective of the merits of their conflict.

None the less, containment relies less than resolution on the constraints and assurances of membership. Deterrence does – sometimes though not infallibly – deter, even when the deterred are united in hatred of the deterrer. But acute problems arise when the regulating agency, whatever it be, has to seek both resolution and containment at the same time. The attitudes involved are deeply at variance.

In the perspective of history it is possible sometimes to see the two techniques as complementary. Between 1815 and 1845 political discontent in Britain was 'contained' largely by force and an odious spy system. Yet in the time thus bought, forces more favourable to resolution were gathering strength, some in reaction to the experience of containment. Political reform made its first impact. Industrial development began to diffuse wealth, however narrowly. The dread of the French revolution dropped astern. The next decades, in which resolution would count for a little more, containment for a little less in the conflicts of the nation, owed something to the darker decades immediately before.

But generally speaking, techniques of resolution and containment are largely inconsistent. The would-be regulator, in his seat of power, has in one hand a bunch of techniques for resolution, all involving time, none predictable in effect and all vulnerable to the actions of those who do not wish them to succeed. In the other hand he holds a bunch of techniques for containment, usually quicker in their action, capable of being used unilaterally, unavoidable against some kinds of attack, yet liable, however carefully used, to communicate a message inconsistent with his efforts at resolution. The situation changes unpredictably and each use of either set of techniques will change it further. But somehow the total sum of conflict must be kept within that elusive threshold which I have called breakdown and which it is now time to consider.

7 The concept of stability

Men in a ship at sea have a common and usually overriding interest in keeping afloat. This requires them both to combine their skills and to moderate their conflicts. There is an analogy, useful though imperfect, between them and the members of each of those 130-odd political societies into which the population of the planet is at present organized and even between their societies *inter se*.

Merely to state the analogy is to awaken suspicion and dissent; for so many crimes and follies have been committed in the name of national security. But this makes it only the more important to examine carefully the meaning and conditions of national coherence.

A ship's company, like a political society, can quarrel about many things; about the way rights, powers and duties are distributed between different posts on board; about who holds these posts, especially the top one, and how they are appointed; about the wisdom and humanity of the orders given; even about where the ship should go. These are also the main subjects of political dispute. Furthermore, men at sea, as on shore, can have all sorts of personal quarrels which have nothing to do with the way the ship is managed, though they may greatly disturb its management.

They seldom disagree about the importance of keeping the ship afloat or deliberately sink it just to spite their fellows. But in the course of a conflict they may easily take risks with it which, to a less involved observer, seem calculated to do no less.

A ship's company, like a political state, is not alone upon the waters of the world. Other ships share them, importing the hazards of accidental collision or even wilful attack and the mutual support of shared information and sometimes succour. Cogent standards govern their mutual behaviour both in avoiding hazard and in rendering help. But the internal relations which make each ship a viable entity are different from and more comprehensive than the external relations which these standards regulate; and any freedom of action which any of them has depends on those inner relations which keep it viable.

The political societies of the world are far more dependent on each other than ships in even the most crowded waterways; they have far less cogent standards for regulating their mutual relationships; they lack much more conspicuously the degree of co-ordination that they need, largely because they are internally much less well organized. Yet it is timely to insist that with all their imperfections they provide today the highest level of general regulation that exists among the human populations of the globe. The nation state may be inept and inadequate but it exists; and for the next thirty years at least most of the important regulative decisions of mankind will necessarily be taken by these authorities, if taken at all. Moreover, the men who will take them and those who will obey them or rebel against them are men alive today, being formed now by the social pressures, the political horizons and the educational systems which today has inherited from the day before yesterday. I make no apology, therefore, for considering conflict containment at the level of the state.

One other comparison. A ship's company is unified largely by the situation of being at sea and by the system of rules and roles which governs the working of ships generally and which they may have learned on other ships. They do not need to know each other well or to be linked by close personal bonds. Situation, rule and role are sufficient to unite them in a self-regulating system which may show the highest sensitivity and endurance. The same is true of other human organizations, including political societies, except that the unifying situation is often less exacting or less realized. It may be masked by internal conflict, by ignorance, by indifference or by mistake. A 'unifying common situation' is worse than useless if it is misconceived. Masefield ends one of his early sea poems –

I saw a ship a-sinking, a-sinking, a-sinking,
with glittering sea water a-splashing on her decks,
with seamen in her spirit room, singing songs and
                                                    drinking,
pulling claret bottles down and knocking off the necks.
The broken glass was chinking as she sank among the
                                                    wrecks.

This image of a unifying but illusory common situation is more familiar in political societies than on ships at sea.

The analogy is imperfect in many ways; but some of these intensify, rather than mute the features I have noted. A ship is an artificial way of enabling a land-living creature to subsist for some time on the barren, unstable surface of the ocean, in which it would otherwise sink and drown. A state is a no less artificial way of enabling that same creature to subsist in a crowded, urban, institutional environment which is no less unnatural. And unlike the ship, which needs to support only brief sorties from the land, the state must support the means of life indefinitely. Food, shelter, the viability of the physical and social environment, all depend on institutional arrangements which are mediated by the state. The state alone legislates; the state alone redistributes income. The state alone determines what share of the national income shall go to provide those ever more essential goods which must be collectively chosen and provided. The rich, no less than the poor, the powerful, no less than the lowly, the employed no less than the unemployed are supported at every turn by right of membership of the political society in which they live. This is even more true of countries like Britain which are both highly developed and densely populated than of other countries, and it grows more important daily.

The institutions of democracy do nothing to change these realities. Their task is to maintain, in governors and governed alike – and everyone shares increasingly in both roles – those constraints and assurances of membership which, through the sum of their influence, keep the volume of conflict within the limits that the society can resolve or contain and thus extend the scope of its coherence. It is ironic that the course of history which has brought us to this degree of inter-dependence should be one which set out to liberate the individual from a different but perhaps not more onerous set of obligations and which, in doing so, has bequeathed to us a set of ideas perfectly calculated to conceal our situation from ourselves and to move us to most inept responses, when at last we begin to see it.

I do not suggest, of course, that our present concept of the political state is the only, the best or even an adequate instrument of political regulation. I insist only that we depend on it for what regulation we have, and must transcend, rather than escape it to attain the greater regulation that we need; and that any interruption in that progress which leaves us without even such regulative powers as we have will threaten the kind of breakdown that I have illustrated by the sinking ship. But the analogy, as I have acknowledged, is not exact.

8 Stability as a political concept

A political society seldom loses its 'order' so completely as a ship that sinks or so irrevocably as an organism that dies. There are many men and women in both West and East Germany today who were adult when Kaiser Wilhelm II committed the German Empire, then less than fifty years old, to the First World

War. They have experienced that war, and the sickness and famine which lasted long after it ended; the creation of the Weimar republic; the disappearance of currency and monetary values in the wild inflation of 1924; the depression, Hitler and the Third Reich, with its new social, political and economic values; the Second World War, bombing, invasion, occupation by three rival foreign powers; partition; and in each half a new political régime, a new currency, new policies ... Four new flags in thirty years! How many new orders, how much disorder – and yet how much of the complex pattern that was there at the beginning is still there at the end, changed but recognizably the same. A political state is a very complex system of systems; we need to comprehend some measure of its complexity, if we are to distinguish its main kinds and degrees of stability.

Let us first draw one basic distinction. An existing order may be criticized for failing to do what it sets out to do or for not even trying to do what its critics think it should. Western capitalism in the 1930s was widely criticized even by its supporters for 'breaking down'. Growth, its supreme criterion, had become recession. Western capitalism in the late 1960s, achieving growth, was criticized for concentrating too much on growth as a criterion and for ignoring distribution, let alone more elusive factors, like the 'quality of life', whose growth should also be its concern. For some critics this failure was evidence that it *could not* achieve these ends and was used as an argument for radically different orders, even for destroying the existing order to make room for an unpredictable successor to grow. For others it was evidence that the existing system had mastered its earlier tasks sufficiently to entertain new ones. Both were conspicuous in USA and both were in marked contrast with British obsession with economic stability. Where Britain was racked with debate about growth rates and the balance of payments, America was racked with debate about national goals. The only stability which emerged there as a political issue was social stability, the threats from crime and violence which were themselves linked to social issues. America felt itself stable enough to have initiative and to exercise choice; Britain, apparently, did not. The difference may have been one of national mood, rather than national achievement or national danger but

165

it illustrates the difference between two types of threatened disorder, which I have called elsewhere[3] innovative and degenerative change.

Every order which men seek to impose on life is a work of art, realizing some values by excluding others. Consequently, none is permanent; each is in time replaced by one which not only accords better with changed circumstances but also does more justice to the values which its predecessor neglected. In the battle between rival orders fighting for realization, the protagonists of each see the other as 'disorder'. But the real issue between them is more akin to an argument about where the ship should be going than to one about how to keep it afloat. It is concerned, in other words, with innovative, rather than degenerative change.

The other kind of disorder – degenerative change – is more typical of the kind of breakdown I am examining. A country which imports half its food may reasonably become obsessively concerned with its balance of payments, once this ceases to be taken for granted. Admitting that even the England of the 1960s had higher ambition than simply to eat, it remains true that all such 'higher, ambitions' even the most inconsistent ones, assume that the people who entertain them will keep alive.

Order is partly hierarchic. Initiative at each level depends on the stability of the level below. Just as ships, however variously manned and employed, operate within the limitations of their physical structure and design, so societies of very different types and achievements depend on and are limited by the stability of their internal relations, political, economic and social. There 'must be' enough production and distribution of necessities to keep people active, whatever their activities. There 'must be' means by which collective decisions can be taken and carried out, whatever the decisions may be. There 'must be' sufficient physical security to enable people to go about their business, however varied their businesses. 'Must be'? Not, of course, in the sense that they necessarily will be. These happy conditions are rare in history; they have often failed, they may fail again. But 'must be' none the less in two more limited senses. 'Must', in that these basic requirements, in so far as they are unmet, set limits to what can physically be done. 'Must' also, in so far as those who suffer when they are unmet (directly or indirectly,

166

personally or sympathetically) see their suffering not as an independent variable but as the unacceptable product of human 'ordering' and thus define it (effectively, even if mistakenly) as breakdown.

This last distinction reminds us that our ways of seeing and valuing our situation are themselves systematically organized and are subject to both innovative and degenerative change. At the beginning of the century, booms and slumps seemed to economists and business men and even politicians to be a necessary and acceptable part of a self-regulating but expanding economic system. It was not disorder but the mechanism by which order was preserved, a typical example of what we should now call an error-controlled system. The depression of the 1930s was seen as breakdown not only because of its severity but because a sufficiently influential part of the population found such 'regulation' unacceptable. In consequence, full employment was added to the goals of the system and Keynsian economics showed the techniques for attaining it. This in turn helped to produce the current form of instability, inflation at a rate which in its turn has passed the limits of the acceptable. But it still awaits its Keynes, perhaps because Keynsian remedies for unemployment can be applied by state action, by 'the governors', whilst inflation requires also some self-regulation by the governed.

This cultural world of concepts and values is itself complex; different classes, occupations, even age groups have their own sub-cultures which unite those who share it and divide them from others. And here too we can distinguish degenerative from innovative change. The problems of societies confused by admixtures of cultures or too rapid change are problems of 'degenerative' disorder. What is called a permissive society is not one which values individuality but rather one which has lost confidence in every standard by which to criticize deviance. The distinction between liberty and licence, so dear to liberal ideology, is possible only in a society where liberty is defined and thus limited by standards unusually widely shared and well accepted – though they are correspondingly unnoticed. Anomie, by contrast, is the felt absence of *any* standard.

I have been pursuing a difference which is elusive but not, I think, merely verbal. Political societies in conflict, like ships' companies even when in mutiny, may validly recognize a threat to some relationships which they have an overriding common interest in preserving; and though the relationship is there, whether they notice it or not, its importance to them is always partly and sometimes wholly given to it by their own sentiment, an aspect of their value system which has its own history and its own validity. Marxists in 1914 were incredulous that the proletarians of Germany, France and Britain flocked to their respective standards – especially perhaps Britain, which imposed no compulsory national service until that war was more than a year old.

The reverse of that picture provides an even more striking example. Gandhi conceived in his own mind, practised in South Africa and demonstrated in India the power of a revolutionary technique, based on the intuition that no government, however strong, can survive, if the governed *quietly* withdraw their tacit consent to its legitimacy – quietly, so as not to challenge authority in the field of force in which alone it is necessarily strong. An Indian writer[4] has pointed out that the doctrine has a corollary which its author may not have foreseen. In a revolution of the usual type, the new rulers, having fought their way into the seats of power, find themselves in control of a society in which even those hostile to them have still the habit of obedience to authority. By contrast, the leaders of a revolution won by the technique of civil disobedience, find themselves directing the affairs of a society which has learned to withdraw legitimacy from authority *as such*. Even their friends have to learn again the habits on which political order rests.

So it remains to consider the concept of authority and its relation to order.

9 The concept of authority

In its anthropological sense, an authoritarian society is one in which authority does not have to be enforced, because it is accepted. Such authority need not be centralized. A simple organization which is authoritarian in this sense, yet in which authority is widely diffused is familiar to us, as an extreme example, in the football team. The immensely refined co-ordination of the players is achieved without the giving of any orders, and the chief responsibility for action passes as quickly as the ball. Each player get his instructions from the situation; one of the conditions which make it possible is that the whole field of possible relevance is visible to every player. Within this field each player can distinguish the swiftly changing situations which make demands on him, his team mates and the opposing team; and because all share a common training and a common objective, each can guess, usually with near-certainty, how each of the others will see his situation and what he will try to do about it. Common experience has also built up in each a sense of obligation to do what the situation requires of him and the confident expectation that all his fellows will do the same. These are the conditions which make it possible for these men to combine with such precision in situations which change so fast.

A tribal hunting expedition co-ordinates its activities in the same way and depends on the same conditions.

Antiquity has handed down to us another and very different model of authority, the centralized authority whose orders are implemented by successive lower hierarchies of subordinates. This model originated in the empires of antiquity, where most of the energy was supplied by slaves or subjects temporarily conscripted for labour. Slave labour notoriously needs to be both 'driven' and 'directed'. Thus there appears to be a double antithesis between a football team and the organization that built the pyramids. The first needs neither driving nor directing; the second needs both.

The antithesis is not so sharp as it looks. The player is 'driven' by the demands of the situation, his responses to which have many sources — habit, personal ambition, enjoyment, the will to win ... A voluntary participant, he would not have gained his place in the team if these together had not given him sufficient 'drive'. The slave, lacking such involvement, is driven by the demands of another situation created for him by his master, largely by threat. Similarly, the player is directed by information derived from the field, the slave by information supplied by his master.

Theorists of business organization today, reacting against the hierarchic models of the past, are busy developing a reticular, or net-like model, more suggestive of the football field than of the pyramid builders. Voluntary participants, sufficiently motivated and informed, should, it is argued, need no further driving or direction or even co-ordination. And since the technology of information is in the ascendant today, a double emphasis falls on the primacy of information.

This change of emphasis is welcome; but it takes more than information to make a football team, let alone a business organization. Even a football game conveys no information to an observer, or even a would-be player who is ignorant of the rules of the game and the roles of the players. And with those ubiquitous determinants, rule and role, the constraints and assurances of membership reappear, as they always do, when we are concerned not merely with information but with meaning. Can information be said to have informed, if the recipient only says – 'So what?'

Participants in a business organization are voluntary in a qualified sense. They have some choice, wide or narrow, in their occupation but they usually have no choice but to have some employment. Members of a political state are in a somewhat different case. They were born into that membership and have much more difficulty and limitation in changing it. Some of the features of their situation are imposed on them by decisions of that society, notably by that distinction between the legal and the illegal which is so fundamental to their relations with other people, with organizations and with the state itself. Can authority, in political societies, no less than in business organizations, be transformed from an hierarchical to a reticular pattern?

No doubt to some extent it can; but the effect is to make it more pervasive and more demanding, even though less oppressive.

Forty years have passed since Chester Barnard[5] distilled from his experience as a business executive a definition of authority which perfectly expresses this reticular conception. Anyone who accepts another's decision without confirming it by his own independent act of judgment accepts that other's authority. An executive accepts his secretary's authority on how to file his personal papers, when he leaves the decision to her. Moreover, he has no real choice in fact and no right to a real choice even in theory. To every position, high or low, there belong decisions which can only be taken by him who sits in that particular seat of power, however lowly.

Authority, then, attaches to positions, is defined by roles and

170

depends on trust, claimed by the holder and accorded by all whom his decisions affect. Have not his 'superiors' the right to check his performance in order to confirm that their trust is not misplaced? They have, for that purpose only and in so far as they can – rigidly limiting qualifications – but each of them has equally the duty of giving, to those who rely on him, whatever their official relation with him, as much opportunity as they can have to confirm that he too merits the confidence which his position claims from them.

This, I believe, is a fair statement of the concept of authority as applied to a reticular organization. Many role holders would not accept its implications. And equally, many of those who are most active in their attack on hierarchic authority seem wholly unconscious of what a fully reticular organization, business or political, would demand *of them*, in particular, of its reciprocal obligation to *trust* and to *earn trust*.

For authority is not eliminated in a reticular organization. It is disseminated; and equally disseminated is the responsibility for trusting and earning trust; the specific trust which is involved in all inter-dependent role-playing and which alone generates the constraints and assurances of membership.

10 The conditions of containment

Containment is a relative term. Subjectively, 'breakdown' in the relations of the contesting parties may range over a wide spectrum from alienation to intense enmity. These subjective thresholds are drawn by the parties to the conflict, usually by one of them; for any of them, by defining the other as an enemy, can usually insist on being so defined himself. Objectively, a complex system may pass some critical point of no return – like the ship in Masefield's poem – without its human constituents being aware of it; but equally, it may pass through many degrees of disorder, any one of which its constituents may define as breakdown. How much violent protest, how many strikes over what issues can a society stand? And equally, from the other viewpoint, how much political dissent, economic distress or social deprivation can be contained by those affected within the currently accepted thresholds governing protest and pressure for change? These questions are answered, however unconsciously, in the course of the endless dialogue which constitutes the political process; and these answers draw the limits of containment.

According to the modest definition of peace which I have adopted, it is the part of those working for peace to keep conflicts within these thresholds so far as may be, and, when they escape, to contain them again, so that the process of resolution may go on.

This is enough to define those who work for peace as enemies in the eyes of those who work for breakdown. Everyone should recognize this unpleasant fact, especially workers for peace, to whom it is least credible, as well as least welcome. It is possible, for good reasons as well as bad, to seek, as an end in itself, that breakdown which will allow a conflict to be fought out. But the worker for peace will be slow to accept such a decision, partly because such simple polarizations are usually the refuge of minds incapable of facing the full implications of their situation, and partly because he believes, rightly, that a world so interconnected and so unstable as ours today can afford very little civil war. What then can be done to increase the scope for containment?

The worker for peace, like everyone else, may have to take sides in such a war and to fight as best he may. But when not so engaged, his tasks are to help define the objective thresholds more precisely and the subjective thresholds more widely.

The case for both is the same. The current situation has been created not merely by accelerating change but by the emergence of one specific and radical change, which is irreversibly altering the situation of men on earth. The essential nature of this is that growth in nearly every dimension has become self-limiting – or rather that its inherently self-imitating nature has become apparent. It can still occur; but its costs can no longer be ignored. Whether in our ecological relation with the planet or in our political or economic or social relations with each other, we cannot ignore the systematic relation which attaches multiple costs to every benefit we seek. The constraints of closer organization are becoming more evident and its enablements more qualified.

Until quite recently our 'environment' was conceived as boundless and independent. It was there to be explored, exploited, modified to suit us or, at the worst, to be 'adapted to';

172

but not to be fostered, tended or served. There was indeed another much closer, much smaller environment, a system of familiar persons, land and resources which offered and claimed membership; but this was a small enclave in a boundless world. Today, the boundless world has shrunk and the world that claims membership has grown. They have coalesced. The net of mutual relations, physical and human, is world wide. The objective thresholds which contain us are far more pressing than before; and subjectively, the act of defining an 'other' as enemy or even alien is far more disturbing and far more costly than it was.

To do so is not on that account less possible or perhaps less logical. Given increasing inter-dependence and increasing mutual limitation, the crowded societies of a crowded earth must *either* develop a sense of common membership far more comprehensive and exacting than they have had or needed or contemplated before *or* they must create distance and independence by allowing conflict to pass the threshold of breakdown and permit them to classify each other as alien or as enemy. Either course will have formidable costs; and no process of logic can decide between these courses – unless it be 'logical' for human beings to choose the more human rather than the less human of the alternatives open to them. Logical or no, he who favours more human, rather than less human solutions will accept the fact that what we value in human societies is created by the constraints and assurances by which they cohere; and he will continue to claim the membership on which these depend, to acknowledge its obligations and to expect them in others; and to uncover, in every conflictual situation, the underlying bond of potential common membership – which may be more comprehensive than any material common interest.

The world to which we are committed by our growing inter-dependence is a world in which individuals will accept the constraints and prize the assurances of membership in many communities, some hierarchically ordered, some overlapping, all to some extent conflicting but none so exclusive as to deny our common membership in the complement of our planetary space ship. Such a world could exist only if its inhabitants were powerfully conditioned to accept it, to desire it and to detect and suppress any threat to it, from dissident groups and individuals no less than from autocratic institutions. It would be a

173

world in which the conditions of communication were prized and protected as highly as past ages have prized and protected the conditions of individual independence. It would be a world unified by a view which may seem austere to us, uncomfortable to the Establishment and perhaps even more uncomfortable for today's rebels against the Establishment. But both, I believe, will have to learn it in the end – unless we leave to our successors, if any, to learn from the history of our failure.

References

1 Bibby, G. (1962), *Four Thousand Years Ago*. Collins. London.
2 I have done so more fully in Vickers, G. (1972), *Freedom in a Rocking Boat*. Penguin Books.
3 Vickers, G., *Freedom in a Rocking Boat*. pp. 124-5.
4 I cannot trace the reference to this publication but I do not wish on that account to appropriate without acknowledgment what seems to me to be an important insight.
5 Barnard, Chester (1938), *The Function of the Executive*.